Cambridge Certificate in Advanced English 3

WITH ANSWERS

Official examination papers from University of Cambridge ESOL Examinations

CAMBRIDGE
UNIVERSITY PRESS

CAMBRIDGE UNIVERSITY PRESS
Cambridge, New York, Melbourne, Madrid, Cape Town, Singapore,
São Paulo, Delhi, Dubai, Tokyo, Mexico City

Cambridge University Press
The Edinburgh Building, Cambridge CB2 8RU, UK

www.cambridge.org
Information on this title: www.cambridge.org/9780521739146

First published 2009
3rd printing 2010

Printed in the United Kingdom at the University Press, Cambridge

A catalogue record for this publication is available from the British Library

ISBN 978-0-521-739139 Student's Book without answers
ISBN 978-0-521-739146 Student's Book with answers
ISBN 978-0-521-739153 Audio CDs (2)
ISBN 978-0-521-739160 Self-study Pack (Student's Book with answers and Audio CDs (2))

Contents

Thanks and acknowledgements

The authors and publishers acknowledge the following sources of copyright material and are grateful for the permissions granted. While every effort has been made, it has not always been possible to identify the sources of all the material used, or to trace all copyright holders. If any omissions are brought to our notice, we will be happy to include the appropriate acknowledgements on reprinting.

FashionUnited for the text on p. 7 'Henri-Lloyd launches women's fashion footwear' from www.fashionunited.co.uk. Reproduced by permission of FashionUnited Worldwide; A & C Black Publishers Ltd for the text on p. 8 'Designing costumes for the theatre' from *Costumes for the stage* by Sheila Jackson. Published by Methuen Drama, an imprint of A & C Black Publishers; Ink Publishing for the text on p. 9 'What's happening in fashion retail?' from 'What next in fashion?' from *EasyJet Inflight Magazine*. Reproduced by permission of Ink Publishing; Independent News and Media Limited for the article on pp. 10-11 'The boat of my dreams' by Tom Cunliffe, *The Independent* 7 January 1999. Copyright © Independent News and Media Limited; Abner Stein for the adapted text on p. 12 'Creative Hurdles' by Jane Smiley, *The Guardian*, 23 May 2006. Reproduced by permission of Abner Stein and the author; Adapted text on p. 33 'Language learning' from www.kurin5hin.org; Hodder Headline and Grove Atlantic for the adapted extract from a novel on p. 34 *Deafening* by Frances Itani. Copyright © 2003 Frances Itani; text on p. 35 'Non-verbal Communication: Where Nature Meets Culture' from www.questia.com; NI Syndication Limited for the adapted text on pp. 36-37 'World Music: Cheikh Lô' by Nigel Williams, *The Times*. Reproduced by permission of NI Syndication; The Orion Publishing Group for the adapted text on p. 38 'Introduction to a book about maps' from *The Map Book* by Peter Barber. Reproduced by permission of Weidenfeld & Nicholson, a division of Orion Publishing Group (London); BBC Wildlife Magazine for the extracts on p. 41 from the *Natural Classic Book Reviews*. Written by Lean, Durrell, Bennett and Pearson. Reproduced by permission of BBC Magazines, Bristol; text on p. 59 'An Actor's Life Story' from www.chicklit.com; The Guardian for the adapted text on p. 67 'Favourite science fiction authors' from 'The war of the words' by Radford, Rogers and Rutherford. *The Guardian* 26 August 2004. Copyright © Guardian News and Media Ltd, 2004; ReadySteadyBook.com for the text on p. 86 'Review of Journalism: A very short introduction' by Ian Hargreaves from http://www.readysteadybook.com/bookreview.aspx?isbn=0192806564. Reproduced by permission of ReadySteadyBook.com and the author, Marty Drury; text on p. 87 'A closer look at the newspaper editorials' from www.rpgamer.com; Roger Bray for the adapted text on pp. 88-89 'Where the landscape will do the walking' from *The Financial Times* 1999. Reproduced by permission of Roger Bray; How To Books Ltd for the text on p. 93 'How to run a shop' from *How to buy and run a shop* by Ian Maitland. Reproduced by permission of How To Books Ltd/Transita Ltd.

Colour section

C1: © Keren Su/Corbis, *bottom right*; Photos for Books/photographersdirect.com, *top*; Peter Frischmuth/Still Pictures, *bottom left*.
C2: © Little Blue Wolf Productions/Corbis, *bottom left*; Romilly Lockyer/The Image Bank/Getty Images, *bottom right*; Nacivet/Taxi/Getty Images, *top*.
C3: © Gary Houlder/Corbis, *bottom right*; © Michael S. Yamashita/Corbis, *centre left*; Peter Cadel/Stone/Getty Images, *top right*; Charly Franklin/Taxi/Getty Images, *centre right*; Hugh Penney Photography/photographersdirect.com, *bottom left*; Topfoto/The Image Works, *top left*.
C4: © Jonathan Blair/Corbis, *top left*; Empics/SportsChrome, *top right*; Topfoto, *bottom*.
C5: Art Directors & Trip/Bob Turner, *bottom*; © David Turnley/Corbis, *top*; Sean Murphy/Stone+/Getty Images, *centre*.
C7: Barros & Barros/The Image Bank/Getty Images, *top left*; Don Smetzer/Stone/Getty Images, *bottom*; Topfoto/The Image Works, *top right*.
C8: Leslie Garland Picture Library/Alamy, *top*; Chris Howes/Wild Places Photography/Alamy, *bottom right*; Rex Features, *bottom left*.
C10: Jerry and Marcy Monkman/EcoPhotography.com/Alamy, *bottom left*; Stockshot/Alamy, *bottom right*; © Atlantide Phototravel/Corbis, *top*.
C11: Leslie Garland Picture Library/Alamy, *top*; Jonathan Smith/Alamy, *bottom right*; Photolibrary Group, *bottom left*.
C12: A1PIX/GrandAngleFoto/photographersdirect.com, *top left*; Empics/AP, *centre right & bottom left*; EDP Pics/K. Tovell/Rex Features, *centre left*; Topfoto/The Image Works, *top right & bottom left*.

Picture research by Sandie Huskinson-Rolfe of PHOTOSEEKERS

Design concept by Peter Ducker

Cover design by David Lawton

The recordings which accompany this book were made at Studio AVP and dsound, London.

Introduction

This collection of four complete practice tests comprises papers from the University of Cambridge ESOL Examinations Certificate in Advanced English (CAE) examination; students can practise these tests on their own or with the help of a teacher.

The CAE examination is part of a suite of general English examinations produced by Cambridge ESOL. This suite consists of five examinations that have similar characteristics but are designed for different levels of English language ability. Within the five levels, CAE is at Level C1 in the Council of Europe's *Common European Framework of Reference for Languages: Learning, teaching, assessment*. It has also been accredited by the Qualifications and Curriculum Authority in the UK as a Level 2 ESOL certificate in the National Qualifications Framework. The CAE examination is widely recognised in commerce and industry and in individual university faculties and other educational institutions.

Examination	Council of Europe Framework Level	UK National Qualifications Framework Level
CPE Certificate of Proficiency in English	C2	3
CAE Certificate in Advanced English	C1	2
FCE First Certificate in English	B2	1
PET Preliminary English Test	B1	Entry 3
KET Key English Test	A2	Entry 2

Further information

The information contained in this practice book is designed to be an overview of the exam. For a full description of all of the above exams including information about task types, testing focus and preparation, please see the relevant handbooks which can be obtained from Cambridge ESOL at the address below or from the website at: www.CambridgeESOL.org

University of Cambridge ESOL Examinations
1 Hills Road
Cambridge CB1 2EU
United Kingdom

Telephone: +44 1223 553997
Fax: +44 1223 553621
e-mail: ESOLHelpdesk@ucles.org.uk

The structure of CAE: an overview

The CAE examination consists of five papers.

Paper 1   Reading   1 hour 15 minutes
This paper consists of **four** parts, each containing one text or several shorter pieces. There are 34 questions in total, including multiple choice, gapped text and multiple matching.

Paper 2   Writing   1 hour 30 minutes
This paper consists of **two** parts which carry equal marks. In Part 1, which is **compulsory**, input material of up to 150 words is provided on which candidates have to base their answers. Candidates have to write either an article, a letter, a proposal, or a report of between 180 and 220 words.

In Part 2, there are four tasks from which candidates **choose one** to write about. The range of tasks from which questions may be drawn includes an article, a competition entry, a contribution to a longer piece, an essay, an information sheet, a letter, a proposal, a report and a review. The last question is based on the set books. These books remain on the list for two years. Look on the website, or contact the Cambridge ESOL Local Secretary in your area for the up-to-date list of set books. The question on the set books has two options from which candidates **choose one** to write about. In this part, candidates have to write between 220 and 260 words.

Paper 3   Use of English   1 hour
This paper consists of **five** parts and tests control of English grammar and vocabulary. There are 50 questions in total. The tasks include gap-filling exercises, word formation, lexical appropriacy and sentence transformation.

Paper 4   Listening   40 minutes (approximately)
This paper consists of **four** parts. Each part contains a recorded text or texts and some questions including multiple choice, sentence completion and multiple matching. There is a total of 30 questions. Each text is heard twice.

Paper 5   Speaking   15 minutes
This paper consists of **four** parts. The standard test format is two candidates and two examiners. One examiner takes part in the conversation while the other examiner listens. Both examiners give marks. Candidates will be given photographs and other visual and written material to look at and talk about. Sometimes candidates will talk with the other candidates, sometimes with the examiner and sometimes with both.

Grading

The overall CAE grade is based on the total score gained in all five papers. Each paper is weighted to 40 marks. Therefore, the five CAE papers total 200 marks, after weighting. It is not necessary to achieve a satisfactory level in all five papers in order to pass the examination. Certificates are given to candidates who pass the examination with grade A, B or C. A is the highest. D and E are failing grades. All candidates are sent a Statement of Results which includes a graphical profile of their performance in each paper and shows their relative performance in each one.

For further information on grading and results, go to the website (see page 5).

Test 1

PAPER 1   READING (1 hour 15 minutes)

Part 1

You are going to read three extracts which are all concerned in some way with fashion. For questions **1–6**, choose the answer (**A**, **B**, **C** or **D**) which you think fits best according to the text. Mark your answers **on the separate answer sheet**.

Henri-Lloyd launches women's fashion footwear

Henri-Lloyd, the UK sailing clothes brand, is launching a new women's fashion footwear collection. Spanning eight styles in a multitude of colourways, the collection is deemed to be modern and sporty, a bit like the brand itself. According to the company's commercial director, Graham Allen, the women's line is very much a response to consumer and retailer demand. 'It is a really exciting move for us and is a natural extension of our existing men's footwear business,' he says.

Hailed as 'essential staples in the wardrobe of any actively minded woman', the new collection is designed to encapsulate Henri-Lloyd's spirit of adventure, but with a feminine twist. The collection is designed to target a certain mindset rather than a particular demographic, and pinning the Henri-Lloyd team down to a particular age group can be tricky.

The company prides itself on its pioneering styles, aiming to produce the highest quality products with strong functionality and design. Ongoing involvement with the BMW ORACLE racing team has helped cement its technical marine roots with fashion. Outside the UK, Henri-Lloyd's biggest export markets are Italy, Sweden and the USA. The brand can be found in 2,006 stores in 23 countries worldwide.

1   What point is being made about the new collection of shoes?

    A   They are intended to appeal specifically to younger women.
    B   They represent a departure in style from the company's clothes.
    C   They fit well with the company's established image.
    D   The initial idea for them came from within the company.

2   What idea is repeated in the text?

    A   the company's clever use of technical associations
    B   the image of the shoes as practical and stylish
    C   the forward-looking nature of the men's footwear line
    D   the widespread availability of the shoes

Extract from a book on designing costumes for the theatre

Two important considerations when designing historical, or 'period', costumes are shape and colour. Whereas it is possible to eliminate the colour aspect by designing in black, white and grey – as in the early days of television – it is impossible to create a costume which has no shape. Costumes with bad or weak shapes are all too common and it is necessary to train the eye to select what is telling and pertinent and to incorporate these elements into the design. This chapter sketches the changing shape of period clothes; but it should not be thought that the consideration of shape applies only to historical dress – it is just as important when designing a comedy horse or a spaceman's costume, neither of which are in any way related to the historical scene.

The drawings I have made show people from the early medieval period to the 1930s. It must be understood that I have tried to select figures which will show
line 13 fairly clearly the progression of costume style. Transitional styles – often very
line 14 interesting, I fully acknowledge – have necessarily had to be left out. Change of shape is affected by the social history of the period, the availability and discovery of fabrics and the human desire for change. The period covered is indeed a large one, but it must be appreciated that in the early days fashion, and therefore shape, changed very slowly; this has accelerated until today fashion changes almost yearly.

3   What point is the writer making about costume design?

A   Even experienced designers can make mistakes with the shape of a costume.
B   Stage costume designers should beware of using bright colours.
C   The advice given is also relevant to non-theatrical designers.
D   Shape is a potentially more problematic issue than colour.

4   When she uses the phrase 'often very interesting, I fully acknowledge' (lines 13–14), the writer is

A   anticipating a possible criticism from readers.
B   rectifying an omission.
C   admitting that her analysis is necessarily imperfect.
D   accepting that her views are rather traditional.

What's happening in fashion retail?

According to UK prediction consultant Tim Harvey, 'The emerging shopping culture is one that values quirky individuality. We want things that look more distinctive and less mass-produced, that have content and meaning specific to us.' At present we can see large chain stores struggling to create an intimate space within their vast warehouse-like shopping emporiums and win back disgruntled customers. Even Clothes4U are developing a boutique-style environment, with a designer range sold in selected stores from a screened-off area. On the other hand, the news that computer chip technology to aid colour co-ordination – a top beeps if it doesn't match your choice of trousers or skirt – is to be brought in by the company for their mainstream lines, is a declaration of how far off the mark they have strayed from understanding what shopping is all about.

Unfortunately, a huge disparity has emerged in the levels of service. And service is where retailers can add value to the experience of shopping for clothes, because, where matters of image are concerned, buying clothes requires a certain amount of emotional involvement. More than the mere removal of garments in a cramped changing room, most of us invest the new clothes we try on with the ability to augment confidence or bolster self-esteem. Clever retailers know how potentially therapeutic any shopping trip is and can train staff to understand the anxieties we bring to the dressing room mirror.

5   What does the writer say about Clothes4U?

   A   Their use of new technology is attracting more customers.
   B   Their judgement is not always sound.
   C   They have failed to address a change in the world of fashion.
   D   They are unwisely moving to specialist markets.

6   The writer implies that successful clothes shops encourage their staff to

   A   allow customers room to make their own choices.
   B   show an interest in the lives of their customers.
   C   find a point of similarity between themselves and their customers.
   D   exploit their customers' insecurities.

Part 2

You are going to read an extract from a magazine article about boat design. Six paragraphs have been removed from the extract. Choose from the paragraphs **A–G** the one which fits each gap (**7–12**). There is one extra paragraph which you do not need to use. Mark your answers **on the separate answer sheet**.

THE BOAT OF MY DREAMS

The best boat design should combine old and new, says Tom Cunliffe. And he put it into practice in his own craft, 'The Westerman'.

This week, the Summer Boat Show in London is resplendent with fine yachts, bristling with new technology. Nearly all are descendants of the hull-shape revolution that took place 25 years ago. By contrast, my own lies quietly on a tidal creek off the south coast. She was designed last year but, seeing her, you might imagine her to be 100 years old and think that her owner must be some kind of lost-soul romantic.

7	

It has to be said, however, that despite being an indispensable tool in current design methods and boat-building practice, sophisticated technology frequently insulates crews from the harsh realities of maritime life. These are often the very realities they hoped to rediscover by going to sea in the first place.

8	

The occasional battle with flapping canvas is surely part of a seaman's life. And for what purpose should we abandon common sense and move our steering positions from the security of the aft end to some vulnerable perch halfway to the bow? The sad answer is that this creates a cabin like that of an ocean liner, with space for a bed larger than the one at home.

9	

Her sails were heavy, and she had no pumped water, no electricity to speak of, no fridge, no central heating, no winches, and absolutely no electronics, especially in the navigation department, yet she was the kindest, easiest boat that I have ever sailed at sea.

10	

The Westerman has never disappointed me. Although Nigel Irens, the designer, and Ed Burnett, his right-hand man, are adept with computer-assisted design programs, Irens initially drew this boat on a paper napkin, and only later transferred his ideas to the computer. After this had generated a set of lines, he carved a model, just as boatyards did in the days of sail. Together we considered the primary embryonic vessel, then fed the design back into the electronic box for modification.

11	

Her appearance is ageless, her motion at sea is a pleasure and her accommodation, much of it in reclaimed pitch pine, emanates an atmosphere of deep peace. Maybe this is because she was drawn purely as a sailing craft, without reference to any furniture we might put into her. That is the well-tried method of the sea.

12

has all the benefits of a glass fibre boat yet looks like, feels like and sails like the real thing.

Constructed in timber treated with a penetrating glue, she is totally impervious to water. Thus she

---

A It's not that I'm suggesting that sailors should go back to enduring every hardship. It's always been important to me that my boats have a coal stove for warmth and dryness and cosy berths for sleeping. But why go cruising at all if every sail sets and furls itself?

B Back on land, however, it is a sad fact that the very antiquity of classic boats means that they need a lot of looking after. When I had a bad injury to my back, I realised that my 15-year love affair with her had to end. Searching for a younger replacement produced no credible contenders, so I decided to build a new boat from scratch.

C In her timeless serenity, she is the living proof that it works; that there is no need to follow current fashions to find satisfaction, and that sometimes it pays to listen to the lessons of history.

D The next version was nearly right and by the time the final one appeared, the form was

perfect. The completed boat has now crossed the North Atlantic and has won four out of her first six racing starts.

E At the same time, having lived aboard an ancient wooden beauty in the early seventies, it's easier to understand more of this area of the mechanics. My designer, for example, knows more about the ways of a boat on the sea than anyone I can think of.

F Perhaps I am, though I doubt it. This boat has benefited from all the magic of old-fashioned boat design, but it would have been a much harder job without the advances of modern know-how.

G For me a boat should always be a boat and not a cottage on the water. When I bought an earlier boat, Hirta, in which I circumnavigated Britain for a TV race series, the previous owner observed that she had every comfort, but no luxury. During my long relationship with her, *Hirta* taught me how wise he was.

New horizons: Tom Cunliffe on board 'The Westerman'

Part 3

You are going to read a magazine article about a writer. For questions **13–19**, choose the answer (**A**, **B**, **C** or **D**) which you think fits best according to the text. Mark your answers **on the separate answer sheet**.

Creative Hurdles

Jane Smiley describes her experiences as a writer.

In 2001, the year I turned 52, I started work on *Good Faith*, my thirteenth novel. But when I sat down at the computer to write, my heart would sink. There were about 125 pages to go, and I felt like I had wandered into a dark wood. I was afraid. Physical fears were all too familiar for me – I had been wrestling with them my whole life, but when I sat down at my computer and read what I had written the day before, I felt something different – a recoiling, an unexpected aversion. Oh, this again. This insoluble, unjoyous labour of mine. What's the next sentence, even the next word? I didn't know, and if I tried something I suspected it would just carry me farther down the wrong path, would be a waste of time or, worse, prolong an already prolonged piece of fraudulence.

I came up with all sorts of diagnoses for my condition. The state of the world was tempting but I refused to be convinced. The problem with the novel was not outside myself, or even in my link to human consciousness. Perhaps, I thought, it was my own professional history. Between 1977 and 1993, I had lived what was essentially a domestic life – husband, house, and children, plus university teaching. I hummed along, apparently performing my professional and family duties, but really half absent. Always my mind was elsewhere, pondering whatever novel I was writing. Only at night did I exert myself to stop thinking about my ideas for the novel, because if I allowed them in, I wouldn't be able to sleep.

As a teenager I had been obsessed with horses. In 1993, they became a large part of my life once again – to the extent that they displaced my novels. My preoccupation went through several stages, including those of feverish research and cultivating equestrians, trainers and vets. Writing novels was now something I did when I was sitting at my desk, but not when I was cooking dinner or driving the children to school. Then I had a riding accident and broke my leg, so there was nothing really to do other than write. And then came *Horse Heaven*, which was, for me, book heaven. I had successfully combined my two obsessions, and the result was pure joy. As far as I was concerned the book had only one flaw – that its composition ended so soon.

But had the literary ruminations the horses had displaced been essential to novel writing? The answer to this depended on one's theory of creativity. I hadn't ever had much of a theory of creativity beyond making a cup of tea and sitting down at the typewriter or computer. The first and last rules were, get on with it. But perhaps that getting on with it that I had taken for granted for so many years was dependent upon those half-attentive ruminations during breadmaking and driving down the road? Or maybe teaching had stimulated me? Week after week for 14 years I had expounded about writing, given tips, analysed student stories, come up with suggestions, fielded questions. Subconsciously, I had *line 27* worked out solutions for my own writing from rules I blithely laid down in class. I wasn't doing that any more, either. Nor was I reading much fiction. In addition to not thinking much any more about my own novels, I didn't think much any more about anyone else's novels.

It was time to face my real fear – that my book wasn't much good. I had confidently stated more than a few times that the execution of a good novel was inherent in the idea from the first. But that was when I was certain all my ideas were good. It may come as a surprise to those who don't care for my work that I'd hardly ever doubted the significance of any idea I'd had, and I'd had very few ideas. I'd written 12 finished works. I'd had 14 ideas. The structure of all of my completed novels was fairly apparent to me from the beginning, and I had written with an increasing energy and sense of direction as I went through the rough draft.

At the halfway mark, I stopped and read through what I had written of *Good Faith*. It was more interesting than I had thought. The energy of that realisation pushed me forward another 60 pages. By now, though, I was looking for terminal symptoms. One day I waited for inspiration, got some, went off in a completely new direction, then had second thoughts the next day and tried something new. This was a symptom, indeed, a symptom that I didn't know what in the world I was doing or where I was going, and it was way too late in the game for that. My heart sank. No, my flesh turned to ice. No, my stomach churned. No, all I did was close the file on my computer, and walk away. But that was very bad. I decided to read a hundred novels.

13 In the first paragraph, what was the writer's reaction to writing her thirteenth novel?

    A She was concerned that the book would be overlong.
    B She was surprised by her feelings about writing the book.
    C She was worried that the book would not appeal to readers.
    D She thought the deadline set for the book was unachievable.

14 It becomes clear in the second paragraph that the writer

    A was too easily distracted.
    B was tempted to give up writing.
    C was struggling to remember what she had written.
    D was uncertain as to what had led to her situation.

15 What does the writer say about her book *Horse Heaven*?

    A It had been necessary to do a lot of research for the book.
    B She had got ideas for the book throughout the day.
    C A lot of the people she had met featured in the book.
    D She had wanted to continue working on the book for longer.

16 What is the purpose of the writer's questions in the fourth paragraph?

    A to try and clarify what enabled her to write
    B to understand her preoccupation with horses
    C to convince others of her theory of creativity
    D to establish how her routine had been stressful

17 What point does the writer illustrate in her reference to 'rules I blithely laid down' in line 27?

    A She had been too critical of her students' work.
    B She had not read enough books during this period.
    C She had been mistaken in her approach to teaching.
    D She had not appreciated how she benefited from such things.

18 How does the writer defend her first twelve books against potential criticism?

    A They were technically well written.
    B Many people could relate to the books.
    C They were written with complete confidence.
    D The ideas behind the books were very original.

19 What does the writer say in the final paragraph about her attempts to finish the book?

    A She was feeling too unwell to continue.
    B Changing her mind at this stage was unhelpful.
    C The half she had already done needed to be rewritten first.
    D She had to increase the amount of time she spent writing.

Part 4

You are going to read an article about clock radios. For questions **20–34,** choose from the sections (**A–E**). The sections may be chosen more than once.

Mark your answers **on the separate answer sheet**.

In which section are the following mentioned?

a tester admitting that he did not trust any type of alarm clock	**20**
a tester later regretting having touched the controls	**21**
a tester approving of a model because of its conspicuous appearance	**22**
the testers being able to operate the model without reference to the manual	**23**
a tester's praise for a model despite the existence of a technical fault	**24**
doubts about the reliability of a model because of the design of an additional feature	**25**
the testers feeling positive about their success in getting the model to work	**26**
doubts about whether anyone would wish to follow certain instructions from the manual	**27**
an explanation of why companies had started to make better radios	**28**
the intended market for the model being apparent from its design	**29**
a tester realising that he had drawn the wrong conclusion about a particular feature	**30**
the testers agreeing on the usefulness of a particular feature	**31**
an additional feature which made the price seem competitive	**32**
uncertainty over whether the radio controls had been set in the correct sequence	**33**
a tester's reaction to the imprecision of the alarm	**34**

SOUND THE ALARM

Stuart Harris reports

Many of us listen to the radio when we get up in the morning and most of us also require some external means to persuade us to get out of bed. Thus we have the clock radio. But how do you pick a good one? Our panel, which consisted of myself plus the inventor Tom Granger and the broadcaster Paul Bridges, tested five currently available.

A

The 'dual alarm function' that is advertised with this model does not allow you, as I first supposed, to be woken by the buzzer, snooze a while and then finally be driven out of bed. The instruction booklet advises you to use this function to set two different wake-up times, one for work days and one for weekends, but whose life is programmed to this extent?

Since this model costs more or less the same as the second model tested, the inclusion of a cassette player is quite a bargain – you can fall asleep to your own soothing tapes and wake up to a day without news. We all thought the quality of the radio excellent, too – if only the whole thing was smaller. It's as big as a rugby ball. Paul Bridges said, 'Any clock radio I buy has to leave enough space on the bedside table for my keys, wallet, glasses and telephone. Anyway, I'm completely paranoid and always book a wake-up call in case the alarm doesn't go off.'

B

This model was voted best in the beauty stakes and overall winner. Paul Bridges declared himself 'in love with it', although the clock on the one he tested 'kept getting stuck at 16.00'. I was fascinated by the digital display, with its classy grey numbers on a gentle green background. The wide snooze bar means you can tap it on the edge with your eyes shut. Unfortunately, the smooth undulations and tactile buttons, like pebbles on the beach, encouraged me to run my fingers over them as if they were keys on a piano, which proved my undoing when I finally looked at the 80-page instruction booklet.

The clock has a self-power back-up so you don't have to reset it if someone unceremoniously pulls the plug out in order to use a hairdryer or the vacuum cleaner; this met with unanimous approval. However, we all found it a technical feat to set up – though completing the learning curve made us feel 'cool' and sophisticated.

C

Tom Granger described this model with its extra built-in lamp as 'unbelievably tacky' in the way it's made. 'You have to wrench the funny light out of its socket to get it to work, which makes me wonder about the quality of the rest of it.' He complained that he had to read the instruction booklet twice before he could get it to work; the clock kept leaping from 12.00 to 02.00 so he had to go round again.

The light was certainly hard to position; you would never be able to read by it – it only shines on the clock, which is illuminated anyway. Paul Bridges said he was 'very tickled' by the lamp idea but agreed that the radio was hard to tune. The buzzer is reminiscent of 'action stations' on a submarine and made me feel like hurling the whole thing across the bedroom. Interestingly, however, this model is the third most popular on the market.

D

Clearly aimed at young people, with its brightly coloured casing and matching bootlace strap, this one appealed to the child in Tom Granger and me. 'I would choose this one because it doesn't disappear into the background like the others,' he said. In fact, the traditional design of the controls made it the only one we managed to set up without reading the instruction booklet. Too bad the alarm is allowed a hilarious 20-minute margin for error; the manual notes, 'the alarm may sound about 10 minutes earlier or later than the pre-set time'. Paul Bridges scoffed at such a notion, adding that this model was 'terribly fiddly' and, indeed, 'completely useless'.

E

The simplest and cheapest of all the models tested, this scored points with Tom Granger because it 'seemed very standard and took up little space', but also because it has old-fashioned dial tuning. 'It's more intuitive to set up. With modern push-button tuning you're never really sure if you've pressed all the buttons in the right order so you can't have confidence that the thing will actually work.' He accepted, however, that manufacturers had been obliged to improve the quality of radios because of the advent of button-tuning. I thought the tuning rather crude, as did Paul Bridges, but we agreed that the radio quality was fine. The buzzer on this model certainly works; it succeeded in getting me out of bed in just two beeps!

PAPER 2   WRITING (1 hour 30 minutes)

Part 1

You **must** answer this question. Write your answer in **180–220** words in an appropriate style.

---

1   You are staying in the UK, and your friend Tom has written to you asking you to recommend a computer course.

Read the extract from his letter and the advertisements for two training centres, which you have found in the local newspaper. Then, **using the information appropriately**, write a letter to Tom outlining the advantages of each centre, saying which one you would recommend and why.

> You're good with computers – can you recommend a course for me? I want to learn quickly, not waste time in a big group, and obviously the cost is important! I might not be able to come at the same time each week.
>
> Anyway, let me know soon.
>
> Thanks,
>
> Tom

The Computer Centre

- very good value
- individual tuition
- short and long courses

IT TRAINING CENTRE

- course designed to your needs
- special discounts for students
- beginners to advanced users

Write your **letter**. You should use your own words as far as possible. You do not need to include postal addresses.

Part 2

Choose **one** of the following writing tasks. Your answer should follow exactly the instructions given. Write approximately **220–260** words.

---

2   You read the following announcement in *Sports Watch*, a sports magazine.

> We are conducting an international survey on sports and would like to publish readers' articles which tell us about **both** of the following points:
> * Which **two** sports do you most enjoy watching, and why?
> * Do you think sports in your country have been influenced by sports from abroad? Why? Why not?

Write your **article**.

3   You see the following announcement for a competition in an international magazine.

> # TIME CAPSULE – TO BE OPENED IN 100 YEARS' TIME!
>
> We are preparing a special container designed to be buried underground and opened in 100 years' time. We invite our readers to recommend **three** things to include in this time capsule which represent life and culture today and to say why they would be of interest to people in the future.

Write your **competition entry**.

4   An international research group is investigating attitudes to education in different parts of the world. You have been asked to write a report on education in your country. Your report should address the following questions:

* What are the strengths and weaknesses of education in your country?
* What educational developments would you like to see in your country in the future?

Write your **report**.

5   Answer **one** of the following two questions based on **one** of the titles below.

(a) Adriana Trigiani: *Big Stone Gap*
You have decided to write a review of *Big Stone Gap* for an English language magazine in your country. In your review you should discuss the aspects of the story which you feel would be the most interesting for people from your country. Explain why these aspects would be interesting for them and encourage them to read/watch it for themselves.

Write your **review.**

(b) Dick Francis: *In the Frame*
Your teacher has asked you to write an essay on *In the Frame*. Your essay should discuss the title. Why do you think that the writer chose this title? Comment on the extent to which you feel it was a good choice.

Write your **essay.**

PAPER 3   USE OF ENGLISH (1 hour)

Part 1

For questions **1–12**, read the text below and decide which answer (**A**, **B**, **C** or **D**) best fits each gap. There is an example at the beginning (**0**).

Mark your answers **on the separate answer sheet**.

Example:

0 A amount   **B** figure   **C** sum   **D** quantity

0	A	B	C	D
	—	▬	—	—

The early railway in Britain

In 1830, there were under 100 miles of public railway in Britain. Yet within 20 years, this **(0)** ….. had grown to more than 5,000 miles. By the end of the century, almost enough rail track to **(1)** ….. the world covered this small island, **(2)** ….. the nature of travel for ever and contributing to the industrial revolution that changed the **(3)** ….. of history in many parts of the world.

Wherever railways were introduced, economic and social progress quickly **(4)** ….. . In a single day, rail passengers could travel hundreds of miles, **(5)** ….. previous journey times by huge margins and bringing rapid travel within the **(6)** ….. of ordinary people. Previously, many people had never ventured beyond the outskirts of their towns and villages. The railway brought them **(7)** ….. freedom and enlightenment.

In the 19th century, the railway in Britain **(8)** ….. something more than just the business of carrying goods and passengers. Trains were associated with romance, adventure and, frequently, **(9)** ….. luxury. But the railways **(10)** ….. more than revolutionise travel; they also **(11)** ….. a distinctive and permanent mark on the British landscape. Whole towns and industrial centres **(12)** ….. up around major rail junctions, monumental bridges and viaducts crossed rivers and valleys and the railway stations themselves became desirable places to spend time between journeys.

1   **A**   revolve   **B**   enclose   **C**   encircle   **D**   orbit

2   **A**   altering   **B**   amending   **C**   adapting   **D**   adjusting

3   **A**   route   **B**   way   **C**   line   **D**   course

4   **A**   pursued   **B**   followed   **C**   succeeded   **D**   chased

5   **A**   cancelling   **B**   subtracting   **C**   cutting   **D**   abolishing

6   **A**   reach   **B**   capacity   **C**   facility   **D**   hold

7   **A**   larger   **B**   higher   **C**   bigger   **D**   greater

8   **A**   served   **B**   functioned   **C**   represented   **D**   performed

9   **A**   considerable   **B**   generous   **C**   plentiful   **D**   sizeable

10 **A**   caused   **B**   did   **C**   produced   **D**   turned

11 **A**   laid   **B**   set   **C**   settled   **D**   left

12 **A**   jumped   **B**   stood   **C**   burst   **D**   sprang

Part 2

For questions **13–27**, read the text below and think of the word which best fits each gap. Use only **one** word in each gap. There is an example at the beginning (**0**).

Write your answers **IN CAPITAL LETTERS on the separate answer sheet.**

Example: | 0 | T | O | | | | | | | | | | | | | | | | | |

Enjoy the benefits of stress!

Are you looking forward to another busy week? You should be according (**0**) ..... some experts. They argue that the stress encountered in (**13**) ..... daily lives is not only good for us, but essential to survival. They say that the response to stress, which creates a chemical called adrenalin, helps the mind and body to act quickly (**14**) ..... emergencies. Animals and human beings use it to meet the hostile conditions (**15**) ..... exist on the planet.

The pressures of everyday life are undeniable, but many experts consider the current strategies we use to deal with them to (**16**) ..... inadequate and often dangerous. They believe that (**17**) ..... of trying to manage our response to stress by (**18**) ..... of drugs or relaxation techniques, we must actually exploit stress. Apparently, research shows that people (**19**) ..... create conditions of stress for (**20**) ..... by doing exciting and risky sports or looking for challenges, cope much better with life's problems. Activities of this type (**21**) ..... been shown to create a lot of emotion; people may actually cry or feel extremely uncomfortable. But there is a point (**22**) ..... which they realise they have succeeded and know that it was a positive experience. This is because we learn through challenge and difficulty. That's (**23**) ..... we get our wisdom. Few of (**24**) ..... , unfortunately, understand (**25**) ..... fact. For example, many people believe they suffer from stress at work, and take time off (**26**) ..... a result. Yet it has been found in some companies that by far (**27**) ..... healthiest people are those with the most responsibility. So next time you're in a stressful situation, just remember that it will be a positive learning experience and could also benefit your health!

Part 3

For questions **28–37**, read the text below. Use the word given in capitals at the end of some of the lines to form a word that fits in the gap **in the same line**. There is an example at the beginning (**0**).

Write your answers **IN CAPITAL LETTERS on the separate answer sheet**.

Example:

0	R	E	C	O	G	N	I	T	I	O	N							

Autumn colours

A new term is rapidly gaining (**0**) ..... in the American language – a 'leaf	**RECOGNISE**
peeper' is someone who, in autumn, is on the (**28**) ..... for areas where the	**LOOK**
leaves of deciduous trees have changed colour. In New England, in the	
USA, 'leaf peeping' is big business, generating millions of dollars annually.	
The first report that leaves are changing colour sets off an (**29**) ..... of	**INVADE**
'peepers' thus causing serious obstruction on some roads. Thousands of	
people log on to websites in their (**30**) ..... to find the location of the trees	**EAGER**
that have foliage in the most (**31**) ..... colours.	**GLORY**

The popularity of 'leaf tourism' is well established in New England, and	
the changing colours of autumn provide an annual (**32**) ..... point. The	**TALK**
colours vary from year to year since the (**33**) ..... of the colour is	**INTENSE**
(**34**) ..... on the chemical composition of the dying leaves. After a long dry	**DEPEND**
summer, leaves often turn bright red, while cloudy autumn days will	
produce less spectacular yellows. If climate change leads to (**35**) ..... hot,	**INCREASE**
dry summers in the northern hemisphere, then countries in Europe can	
expect summers not (**36**) ..... those across the Atlantic. They will then enjoy	**LIKE**
a kaleidoscope of (**37**) ..... colour to rival the deep reds and blazing	**SEASON**
oranges seen in New England.	

Part 4

For questions **38–42**, think of **one** word only which can be used appropriately in all three sentences. Here is an example (**0**).

Example:

0 The committee decided to .... the money equally between the two charities.

I can't believe that John and Maggie have decided to .... up after 20 years of marriage.

To serve a watermelon you need to .... it down the centre with a sharp knife.

Example: | **0** | S | P | L | I | T | | | | | | | | | | | | | |

Write **only** the missing word **IN CAPITAL LETTERS on the separate answer sheet**.

---

38 When Erica was trying to complete an important course assignment, she often lost all .... of time, and sometimes forgot to eat.

There is no .... in cleaning the house before the party, but it will certainly need doing afterwards.

Just entering that ancient building gave Simon a real .... of how different life must have been in the past.

39 This is a piece of music which never fails to .... me.

The whole family are planning to .... to Australia later this year.

Next year the club intends to .... the date for the annual dinner to the first Saturday in May.

40 The police are looking for a tall woman with .... hair in connection with the bank raid.

The weather will be .... today although it might rain later this evening.

'I think it would be .... to say that we played very badly today,' the rugby manager said to the journalist.

41 Lenka .... her friends from home when she went away to university.

The car went out of control and just .... hitting a lamp post.

We would have enjoyed the play more if we hadn't .... the first act.

42 Harry has already spent two .... at the college.

The talk was difficult for me to appreciate because the speaker used technical .... I hadn't heard before.

Joe must make sure he understands all the .... laid down in the agreement.

Part 5

For questions **43–50**, complete the second sentence so that it has a similar meaning to the first sentence, using the word given. **Do not change the word given.** You must use between **three** and **six** words, including the word given. Here is an example (**0**).

Example:

0 Fernanda refused to wear her sister's old dress.

NOT

Fernanda said that .... her sister's old dress.

The gap can be filled with the words 'she would not wear', so you write:

Example:	**0**	SHE WOULD NOT WEAR

Write the missing words **IN CAPITAL LETTERS on the separate answer sheet**.

43 There has been a sharp rise in the price of petrol this month.

   RISEN

   The .... this month.

44 Lisa was just about to leave the house when the phone rang.

   POINT

   Lisa was .... the house when the phone rang.

45 Tom's company had less success with its exports this year.

   SO

   Tom's company was .... with its exports this year.

46 A number of sporting events had to be cancelled owing to the bad weather.

LED

Bad weather .... of a number of sporting events.

47 When it comes to computer games, Gareth is a real expert.

CONCERNED

As ...., Gareth is a real expert.

48 Carlos really should get someone to mend his bike.

HIGH

It's .... his bike mended.

49 Do you think Noelia is likely to win the competition?

CHANCE

Do you think Noelia is in .... the competition?

50 I've been greatly impressed by the way Jasper deals with problems.

MADE

Jasper's way of dealing with problems has

.... me.

PAPER 4   LISTENING (approximately 40 minutes)

Part 1

You will hear three different extracts. For questions **1–6**, choose the answer (**A**, **B** or **C**) which fits best according to what you hear. There are two questions for each extract.

Extract One

You overhear two friends discussing a documentary film about the sea.

1   What do they agree about?

    A   the inappropriate style of the commentary

    B   the high quality of photography

    C   the poor choice of narrators

2   During the discussion, the man reveals his

    A   surprise that wildlife films are so popular.

    B   irritation with environmental issues.

    C   respect for underwater camera crews.

Extract Two

You hear part of a radio interview with a man called Gerald Barton who has travelled extensively.

3   How does Gerald use his website?

    A   to publicise his computer company

    B   to make contact with other travellers

    C   to keep a record of where he's been

4   In each of the countries on his list, Gerald has

    A   visited a well-known location.

    B   engaged with the local culture.

    C   spent a minimum of one night.

Extract Three

You hear part of a radio interview with Sarah Grey, who writes and illustrates children's books.

5 Sarah thinks her books are memorable because of the

    A simplicity of the stories.

    B nature of the pictures.

    C variety of the characters.

6 What is Sarah's opinion of the effect of television on children?

    A It gives them little time for reflection.

    B It stops them using their imagination.

    C It can cause them to be overexcited.

Part 2

You will hear a man called Tom Trueman giving a lecture about golf courses and the environment. For questions **7–14**, complete the sentences.

Golf courses and the environment

The recent popularity of golf resulted from

local success in [**7**   ] events.

A demand for new golf courses attracted

the interest of both [**8**   ] and businessmen.

Many developers made the mistake of building

golf courses to [**9**   ] standards.

Golf courses tend to be used by people who live in [**10**   ]

Some people think that golf courses look too much like [**11**   ]

Trees planted on golf courses are often chosen because they [**12**   ]

Tom suggests that golf courses could also be used as [**13**   ]

Tom would like to see golf courses

integrated into both the [**14**   ] and the local ecology.

Part 3

You will hear part of an interview with two chefs, Jane and Chris, who both won prizes in the National Railway Chef of the Year competition. For questions **15–20**, choose the answer (**A**, **B**, **C** or **D**) which fits best according to what you hear.

---

15 Jane admits that the greatest problem she faced during the competition was having to

    A be original when travelling at speed.
    B produce a meal with so little money.
    C work in a very small space.
    D prepare a meal so quickly.

16 What do both Chris and Jane feel is unique about their work?

    A the close contact with the customers
    B the need to do everything at the same time
    C the opportunity they have to be creative
    D the way they have to focus on the job

17 What do Chris and Jane feel about what they cook on board the train?

    A They approve of the menus provided for them.
    B They are more adventurous than other chefs.
    C They would like to have more freedom of choice.
    D They are happy to adapt their ideas to suit the job.

18 Chris thought being a railway chef would suit him mainly because he'd be able to

    A show his ability to work under pressure.
    B use the skills he had been trained for.
    C do something out of the ordinary.
    D satisfy his love of travelling.

19 What is often Jane's initial reaction when things spill over?

    A She asks another member of staff to help her clear up.
    B She blames the train driver for the accident.
    C She tells herself to keep a closer watch next time.
    D She says nasty things to the other staff.

20 What does Chris say caused his worst disaster?

    A leaving things to burn under the grill
    B dropping the main course on the floor
    C losing his concentration when cooking
    D not keeping an eye on the oven temperature

Part 4

You will hear five short extracts in which people are talking about their future retirement.

TASK ONE

For questions **21–25**, choose from the list **A–H** each speaker's present occupation.

TASK TWO

For questions **26–30**, choose from the list **A–H** what each speaker is looking forward to doing when they retire.

While you listen you must complete both tasks.

A	actor
B	doctor
C	architect
D	farmer
E	teacher
F	accountant
G	judge
H	journalist

A	travelling to other countries
B	sleeping longer
C	taking exercise
D	spending time with friends
E	improving their garden
F	reading widely
G	taking up an artistic hobby
H	learning a language

Speaker 1		21
Speaker 2		22
Speaker 3		23
Speaker 4		24
Speaker 5		25

Speaker 1		26
Speaker 2		27
Speaker 3		28
Speaker 4		29
Speaker 5		30

PAPER 5 SPEAKING (15 minutes)

There are two examiners. One (the interlocutor) conducts the test, providing you with the necessary materials and explaining what you have to do. The other examiner (the assessor) is introduced to you, but then takes no further part in the interaction.

Part 1 (3 minutes)

The interlocutor first asks you and your partner a few questions. The interlocutor asks candidates for some information about themselves, then widens the scope of the questions by asking about, e.g. candidates' leisure activities, studies, travel and daily life. Candidates are expected to respond to the interlocutor's questions, and listen to what their partner has to say.

Part 2 (a one-minute 'long turn' for each candidate, plus 30-second response from the second candidate)

You are each given the opportunity to talk for about a minute, and to comment briefly after your partner has spoken.

The interlocutor gives you a set of pictures and asks you to talk about them for about one minute. It is important to listen carefully to the interlocutor's instructions. The interlocutor then asks your partner a question about your pictures and your partner responds briefly.

You are then given another set of pictures to look at. Your partner talks about these pictures for about one minute. This time the interlocutor asks you a question about your partner's pictures and you respond briefly.

Part 3 (approximately 4 minutes)

In this part of the test you and your partner are asked to talk together. The interlocutor places a new set of pictures on the table between you. This stimulus provides the basis for a discussion. The interlocutor explains what you have to do.

Part 4 (approximately 4 minutes)

The interlocutor asks some further questions, which leads to a more general discussion of what you have talked about in Part 3. You may comment on your partner's answers if you wish.

Test 2

PAPER 1   READING (1 hour 15 minutes)

Part 1

You are going to read three extracts which are all concerned in some way with communication. For questions **1–6**, choose the answer (**A, B, C** or **D**) which you think fits best according to the text. Mark your answers **on the separate answer sheet**.

Language Learning

I was inspired to describe my approach to language learning after reading a book on the subject by Tim Barnham. The method he describes is very similar to the one that I use, though I take issue with a couple of his suggestions, and I think his method needs to be updated for the internet age. Nevertheless I recommend the book highly, as it's full of good suggestions. Please note I'm not an expert. I can only comment on my own experiences, and how some tech know-how has helped me pursue my chief pleasure in life: learning languages.

I generally take the internet for granted as an important tool in my daily life, but I still have those 'wow!' moments every now and then. When I'm corresponding, talking or video-chatting with a person on the other side of the world, learning about their culture or what they eat for breakfast, the power of technology is really driven home to me. This experience goes completely hand-in-hand with using the net to learn a language; it's what the net is all about.

1   What is the writer's main purpose in the first paragraph?

    A   to describe which technology skills helped him learn languages
    B   to say which part of Barnham's book impressed him most
    C   to indicate how he benefits from learning a language
    D   to explain his motivation for writing the article

2   What does the writer say about the internet in the second paragraph?

    A   He wishes that he was able to make better use of it.
    B   He cannot understand how he once managed without it.
    C   He is not always aware of how useful he finds it.
    D   He dislikes how important it has become in his daily life.

Extract from a novel

Chapter One

There are eleven other children in Grania's class. Eight of them know sign language. Grania soon learns that even though she is encouraged every day to use her voice she is barely understood. She resolves to keep her voice inside, not to let it out. But her teacher, Miss Amos, won't settle for that. She taps Grania on the shoulder, watches her lips, brings Grania's attention back to her own lips to see the shapes of the words and to practise them. She instructs Grania in the single-hand alphabet, which Grania, already knowing her printed letters, has no trouble learning. She also shows her how to use the signing space in front of her neck and upper chest.

Outside of class, the other children signal to one another with animation. Grania sends signals out slowly from her body, but she is frustrated by the flap and flurry of hands that face her when signals try to come back in. At times she sees nothing more than a rapid blur. Instead, she focuses on lips, as she had done at home. But in class, her teacher wants more: she wants Grania to see that a word is about to form, to guess what it will mean. This works in slow motion with Miss Amos, whom Grania now tries to please, but away from the classroom the other children expect her to understand not lips but hands, and at their speed. If Grania does not understand, she is left out.

3   What does the reader learn about Grania's teacher?

    A   She thinks that Grania must express herself better with her hands.
    B   She expects Grania to make rapid progress.
    C   She spends most of her time with Grania.
    D   She will not allow Grania to remain silent.

4   What does the writer suggest about the other children in Grania's class?

    A   They have limited patience with Grania's difficulties.
    B   They are jealous of Grania's relationship with the teacher.
    C   They mock Grania when her use of sign language is unclear.
    D   They are reluctant to include Grania in any of their conversations.

Non-verbal Communication: Where Nature Meets Culture

The search for the biological foundation of human culture inevitably leads to non-verbal communication. Intuition suggests that such communication has been an essential element of the evolution of humans as social beings. Without it, the diversity and sophistication of today's social systems would be unimaginable. However, there is the opposite hypothesis that the evolution of non-verbal communication may in part be the result of our being thoroughly social entities: the social nature of humans may have amplified the evolution of
line 8 a capacity we share with other primates but developed to a degree unequalled by any other species.

As far as language is concerned, these issues have been subject to fascinating research in linguistics, biological anthropology and other fields. However, the fundamental question of what led to humans becoming social beings and thus, ultimately, the basis of human culture, remains contested between the disciplinary territorial claims of biology and the social sciences. Quite obviously, the presumed interdependence of the evolution of non-verbal communication as a biological function and the evolution of its significance for human culture calls for an interdisciplinary effort to explore the processes involved. One promising approach is the study of similarities and differences of non-verbal communication among humans and non-humans (above all, primates).

5   What does 'a capacity' in line 8 refer to?

   A   biological foundation
   B   non-verbal communication
   C   intuition
   D   social nature

6   What does the writer say about the development of humans as social beings?

   A   Its causes are disputed.
   B   Its significance is underestimated.
   C   Little research has been carried out into the processes involved.
   D   The role played by non-verbal communication is misunderstood.

Part 2

You are going to read an extract from a magazine article about music. Six paragraphs have been removed from the extract. Choose from the paragraphs **A–G** the one which fits each gap (**7–12**). There is one extra paragraph which you do not need to use. Mark your answers **on the separate answer sheet**.

WORLD MUSIC: CHEIKH LÔ

Cheikh Lô's eclectic music is inspired by African rhythms, salsa and pop, says Nigel Williamson.

The man who has just made the best world music album of the year is sitting on a rocky outcrop overlooking the Atlantic Ocean, his hair blowing gently in the African breeze. We are only a kilometre from the centre of Dakar but the bustling Senegalese capital seems a world away. 'I come here in the middle of the night when I need to be alone,' says Cheikh Lô.

7

Now established as one of the most exciting names in world music, he has just returned after a week spent promoting his latest album, which was co-produced by his friend and mentor N'Dour and the record manager Nick Gold.

8

The resulting blend of sounds is warm and lyrical, relaxed yet passionate, a kaleidoscope of apparently simple rhythms that build into complex and mesmerising patterns. Yet, despite this talent, Lô's passage has not been easy and he has had to wait until his forties for recognition. Born in a village in Burkina Faso, he grew up speaking the tribal languages of Wolof and Bambara and hearing traditional African music played.

9

By the time he was a teenager the international language of pop music had infiltrated village life, not only in assimilated local styles but in American forms too. 'I saw American and British singers performing in Africa. I learnt to play Beatles songs on the guitar. So my influences were African, salsa and pop.'

10

And that was what he continued to do. A few years later he migrated to Paris, home to many African musicians, and spent two years playing sessions there. 'I was a studio drummer, I played in a French band and in another reggae band. It was a confusing period. There was so much to learn and I had no money.'

11

Yet it was to be five years before they began. First, the enigmatic Lô disappeared for three years. 'Everybody thought I had given up music but I went to study with my spiritual guide,' Lô explains. His faith still lies at the roots of his music.

12

Hence it was late 1996 before the world got to hear Lô's album *Ne La Thiass*. It was a timeless, mostly acoustic affair, whereas the follow-up possesses a tougher, more cosmopolitan feel. Much of the newfound drive and energy comes from the horn arrangements of Pee Wee Ellis. 'When he came to Dakar to work with us it was like a homecoming for everyone,' Lô says.

The last word on Lô goes to his mentor and champion. 'He's got energy and rhythm and he's got his own musical story,' N'Dour says. 'He's the man to take African music to the world.'

A The recording should earn Lô a hearing far beyond the traditional world-music audience. Still rooted in the swaying Senegalese rhythms known as mbalax, it is also laced with funky horns and a touch of Afro-Cuban fire.

B These included the legendary Cuban flautist Richard Egües, who turned out to have been an early hero. 'I fell in love with his music as a kid when I heard him playing with Orquesta Aragon. I had never heard the flute played like that,' Lô says.

C By the time Lô returned with a batch of songs, N'Dour was otherwise engaged, promoting his global hit *Seven Seconds* with singer Neneh Cherry.

D But his older brothers also had access to imported Cuban salsa records. 'We didn't understand what they were singing about but we related to the swing and rhythm,' he says.

E As a result of this exposure, he was able to get a job when he moved to Senegal at the age of 25. There he joined the house band at Dakar's best hotel, *The Savana*, playing drums and singing bland pop for tourists. 'But it was an education in different sorts of music. I didn't go to music school, so I had to learn on the job.'

F So he returned to Senegal, where he finally got to make his first record in 1990, a low-cost cassette of the kind that dominates the African market but which never sees the light of day elsewhere. Eventually N'Dour heard him playing at a Dakar club and offered to produce an album intended to launch Lô on an international stage.

G Lô is a devout man. He is also the possessor of one of the world's great voices. Three years ago on his London debut, *The Times* reviewed the concert under the headline 'First rays of an African star'.

Part 3

You are going to read an extract from a book. For questions **13–19**, choose the answer (**A, B, C** or **D**) which you think fits best according to the text. Mark your answers **on the separate answer sheet**.

Introduction to a book about maps

This book is a celebration of the map in its myriad forms over time. I have attempted to penetrate beneath the sometimes glossy, sometimes plain surface to look at why they came into being, who their creators were and what their relationship was to the society in which they were created. All this effort may seem excessive for an object which for many people is just an ephemeral item of passing need, though there seems always to have been an equal number for whom maps have been an endless source of fascination on scientific, aesthetic, historical and cultural grounds.

Over the past twenty years most people working on the academic study of maps have come to accept the definition formulated in 1987 by Harley and Woodward at the beginning of the first volume of their monumental and still incomplete *History of Cartography* that 'Maps are graphic representations that facilitate a spatial understanding of things, concepts, conditions, processes or events in the human world'. This is the definition I have borne in mind in this book. In 1987, though, it caused some consternation among those who took a more restrictive view of the map as a primarily utilitarian geographical paper object, whose quality was to be assessed primarily in terms of its geometrical accuracy.

This traditional view of the historical development of mapping was propagated primarily by geographers, some of whom had only a passing acquaintance with historical method, with occasional contributions by librarians and map dealers who were anxious to increase popular interest in their area. Historians of discovery also used old maps to illustrate their texts, sometimes doing research into their creation and publication histories. This practice, and the traditional view of geographers, led to a lasting confusion between the history of exploration and the history of cartography which has proved over-restrictive to both, and beneficial to neither.

Geographical researchers tended to view the evolution of mapping in terms of the gradual victory of objective 'truth' and precise scientific method over geographical ignorance. The achievements of national mapping agencies were lauded as the pinnacles of cartographic achievement. The creators of European mapping from before 1500 were condemned, by most academic geographers, as ignorant or at least befuddled, and many of its most appealing aspects dismissed as 'mere decoration'. Meanwhile mainstream historians assumed that maps were the province of academic geographers. In so far as they took any interest, it was in the form of modern historical mapping that clarified their interpretation of the past.

The detailed study of old maps was relegated to local historians and librarians. The typical fruits of their labours were long lists of maps and the different states in which they were to be found. Much of this work was fascinating in its own right and was essential for any further progress. But it was marked by diffidence and quite often a lack of intellectual rigour. It was as if the authors did not have the collective courage to say out loud what their emotions told them loud and clear: that scientific measurement was not the be all and end all of mapping.

It is only in recent years this has radically changed. This is partly due to the increasing awareness of the importance of the visual, as a consequence of the spread of television and the internet, and the ease with which images can be manipulated in a digital environment. But also, thanks to the growing popularity of interdisciplinary studies at university, academic historians of all types began to find that maps sometimes offered perspectives on their subjects that were not possible from other sources. It is accepted that for some purposes, such as navigation and administration, mathematical accuracy did and still does play a major role in cartography. Conversely, the very aspects that tended to be disregarded, such as the distortions and the decoration, become of enormous significance since they can give particularly precious insights into the mentalities of past ages.

line 37   For many enthusiasts, the fascination of maps ironically stems from the fact that they are pieces of fiction. With historical military maps, for example, the truth dawns that the map they are interested in does not accurately depict the shapes of the fields where battles occurred. Yet it has to be that way. Given the impossibility of representing the total reality, with all its complexity, on a flat surface, hard decisions have to be taken as to what features to select for accurate representation. For most of the time, this process of selection is almost instinctive. The mapmaker knows the purpose that he wants his map to serve, and beyond that he is unwittingly guided by the values and assumptions of the time in which he lives.

In order to meet that purpose, the information that is represented will be prioritized by the mapmaker – and not necessarily in accordance with actual geographical size. Even on modern national topographic mapping such features as motorways will be shown far larger than they actually are because they are important to drivers, and users will expect to see them without difficulty.

13 What does the writer suggest about his book in the first paragraph?

    A He found his aims difficult to achieve.
    B Some enthusiasm for the subject may be needed to appreciate it.
    C The presentation of information in it varies in style.
    D Some people will inevitably use it just as a reference source.

14 What does the writer say about Harley and Woodward's definition of a map?

    A It was modified by its creators.
    B It is now thought to be only partially correct.
    C It lacked originality.
    D It has been accepted only gradually.

15 The way that maps were traditionally regarded and used

    A was influenced by academic self-interest.
    B was based on a fundamental falsehood.
    C caused an unfortunate misunderstanding.
    D led to hostile debates in academic circles.

16 What connection does the writer make in the fourth paragraph between geographers and mainstream historians?

    A They both embraced the subject with enthusiasm.
    B They were both sceptical about the value of using older historical maps.
    C They were both concerned that the majority of maps were European in origin.
    D They both accepted that more progress needed to be made.

17 According to the sixth paragraph, what change has come about in connection with maps?

    A Maps have become fashionable in all sections of the media.
    B Their traditional use for navigation is now less widespread.
    C New reasons for producing maps have emerged.
    D Information previously ignored has been given greater prominence.

18 What point is the writer making about maps as 'pieces of fiction' in line 37?

    A This false view has at least increased their popular appeal.
    B Such kinds of map do not have a place nowadays.
    C This unfortunate development needs to be challenged.
    D A totally accurate representation of an area is unachievable.

19 What point is exemplified by the reference to motorways?

    A the mapmaker's subjective perception
    B the mapmaker's eye for detail
    C the mapmaker's recognition of the social context
    D the mapmaker's need to stay constantly up to date

Part 4

You are going to read an article in which four naturalists explain their choice of most inspiring book about the environment. For questions **20–34**, choose from the naturalists (**A–D**). The naturalists may be chosen more than once.

Mark your answers **on the separate answer sheet**.

Which naturalist

says that the book contained a wider range of material than other books he/she owned?	20
says that the human race is often blamed for its destructive relationship with wildlife?	21
says that the book can make the organisation of a particular animal group clear to an observer?	22
explains what motivated him/her to start drawing?	23
describes experiencing a change of mood when reading the book?	24
praises the book for both its use of language and depth of feeling?	25
describes the sensory experiences evoked by the book?	26
thinks the book encouraged greater optimism about a personal skill?	27
mentions an initial reluctance to become involved in investigating environmental issues?	28
attributes the skill of the illustrator to extensive observation?	29
has come into contact with many leading environmental figures through work?	30
attributes the immediate appeal of the book to its illustrations?	31
first read the book at a time when experiencing problems?	32
comments on the illustrator's ability to show animal behaviour through deceptively simple pictures?	33
says that no other book has proved to be as good as the one nominated?	34

Wildlife Books

*We invited four leading naturalists to tell us about the wildlife classic
that has influenced them most.*

A
Geoffrey Lean

At least it wasn't hard to choose the author. As an environmental journalist, one advantage of longevity is that I have had the chance to meet some of the giants who pioneered thinking in the field. Of these, none stood, indeed, still stands, taller than Barbara Ward. I can't think of anyone else more at the heart of environmental issues. She has synthesised her experience of various environmental movements into her own compelling philosophy. Unwillingly 'volunteered' to cover the field, I found, as a young journalist, that she, more than anyone, made it all make sense.

Picking the book was much harder. It could have been *Only One Earth* or *Progress for a Small Planet*. But *The Home of Man* is, to me, Barbara's most important book. Its focus is on the explosive growth of the world's cities, but its canvas is the great themes to which she devoted her life. It is as eloquent and as impassioned a plea as exists for what we would now call 'sustainable human development'. In the hundreds of books I have read since, I have yet to meet its equal.

B
Linda Bennett

When I open the pages of *Signals for Survival* by Niko Tinbergen, I can hear the long calls of herring gulls, recall the smell of the guano in the hot sun and visualise the general hullabaloo of the colony. This book explains superbly, through words and pictures, the fascinating world of animal communication.

Read *Signals for Survival* and then watch any gull colony, and the frenzy of activity changes from apparent chaos to a highly efficient social structure. You can see which birds are partners, where the boundaries are and, later on in the season, whole families can be recognised.

Niko Tinbergen's collaboration in this book with one of this century's most talented wildlife artists, Eric Ennion, was inspirational and has produced a book of interest to anyone with a love of wildlife. His spontaneous style of painting came from years of watching and understanding birds. With just a minimal amount of line and colour, he brings to life how one gull is an aggressor, how another shows appeasement. This is the art of a true field naturalist.

C
Lee Durrell

Most definitely, *My Family and Other Animals* by my husband Gerald Durrell is the book that has had the greatest influence on my life.

I was doing research work into animal vocalisations in Madagascar when I first read the book. I had been there two years and was discouraged by the number of setbacks I was encountering but when, at the end of the day, I opened *My Family and Other Animals* to where I had left off the night before, the world became a brighter place. Animals, people, joy and beauty inextricably woven together – a microcosm of a world worth saving.

Many people say that our species is the worst because of the terrible things we have done to the others. But I like to think back to Gerald as a boy in *My Family and Other Animals*, looking at the world's inhabitants as a whole, a family whose members, be they good, bad or indifferent, are nevertheless so intertwined as to be inseparable. And that is a concept we all need to grasp.

D
Bruce Pearson

A copy of *The Shell Bird Book*, by James Fisher, found its way into my school library shortly after it was first published in 1966. I was drawn to it at once, especially to the 48 colour plates of birds by Eric Ennion, painted, as the jacket puts it, '... with particular skill and charm'. It was those Ennion images which captured my attention.

I already had copies of other bird books and had spent several holidays learning to identify birds. They encouraged me to begin sketching what I saw as an aid to identification. But in *The Shell Bird Book* there was so much more to feast on. As well as the glorious Ennion paintings, there were chapters on migrants and migration, a review of the history of birds in Britain, and, best of all, a chapter on birds in music, literature and art.

It was the broad span of ornithological information and the exciting images that steered me towards being more of a generalist in my appreciation of birds and the natural world. The book made it clear that my emotional and creative response to nature was as valid and as possible as a rational and scientific one. And, as art was a stronger subject for me than maths or physics, I began to see a door opening for me.

PAPER 2 WRITING (1 hour 30 minutes)

Part 1

You **must** answer this question. Write your answer in **180–220** words in an appropriate style.

---

1 During your last holidays, you and your friend, Alex, worked in an international holiday centre organising activities for young children. Tim Allsop, the Manager of the holiday centre, has written to you asking for a report about your experiences.

   Read the email from Alex, together with some notes you have made. Then, **using the information appropriately**, write a report for Tim Allsop, outlining your experiences and making suggestions for improvements.

From:	alex@cas.ac.uk
Subject:	Our holiday experience

It was great to work together, and I enjoyed being with the kids. The social life was good. Pity Toni got fed up and left early – he'd have enjoyed the second week more. At least the food improved and the work got easier, don't you think? . . .

Own notes

- thought I'd be teaching children sports, not art!
- accommodation awful
- only with people from own country
- needed clearer advance information

Write your **report**. You should use your own words as far as possible.

Part 2

Choose **one** of the following writing tasks. Your answer should follow exactly the instructions given. Write approximately **220–260** words.

---

2   There is going to be an international music festival in your area. You have seen the following notice in the local newspaper.

> ## International Music Festival – Judges Wanted.
>
> Can you help? Thousands of groups and musicians have applied to play in our 3-day festival. We need judges to help us decide which groups and musicians to accept.
> If you are interested in working with us, please write explaining:
> * which types of music you think we should have
> * what your own tastes in music are
> * what would make you a good judge.

Write your **letter of application**.

3   Many British students work in another country during their vacation. You have been asked to write the entry on **your** country to be included in a new book called *A Guide to Temporary Jobs Around the World*, covering the following points:

* types of possible jobs and how to find them
* pay and conditions
* advice about possible problems students may face when working in your country.

You should write about 2 or 3 vacation jobs.
Write your **contribution** to the guidebook.

4   Your international college has a lot of sports and arts facilities which students can use in their spare time. There is also a wide range of recreational activities which students can participate in.

You have been asked to write an information sheet which:

* informs the students about all that is available
* points out the benefits of taking up these opportunities
* encourages students to use the facilities and join in the activities.

Write your **information sheet**.

5   Answer **one** of the following two questions based on **one** of the titles below.

(a) Adriana Trigiani: *Big Stone Gap*
Your College Principal has offered a prize for the best English language book report written by someone in the college. You have decided to write a report on *Big Stone Gap*. Your report should focus on what you learnt from the book both about life in general and from the language learning point of view.

Write your **report**.

(b) Dick Francis: *In the Frame*
You have been asked to write an article about *In the Frame* for your college magazine. In your article you should discuss how the hero behaved. To what extent do you admire his behaviour? Would you have behaved in the same way in the different situations in which he found himself?

Write your **article**.

PAPER 3   USE OF ENGLISH (1 hour)

Part 1

For questions **1–12**, read the text below and decide which answer (**A**, **B**, **C** or **D**) best fits each gap. There is an example at the beginning (**0**).

Mark your answers **on the separate answer sheet**.

Example:

0 A journey   **B** travel   **C** route   **D** way

0	A	B	C	D
	▬	▭	▭	▭

Driving from Beijing to Paris

'Every **(0)** ..... begins with a single step.' We might **(1)** ..... this proverb for the annual 16,000 km Beijing to Paris car rally, and say that every rally begins with a turn of the wheel. From China, several hundred courageous men and women will **(2)** ..... out for Paris in pursuit of what, for many, is likely to prove an impossible **(3)** .... Everybody is prepared for the worst and organiser Philip Young expects a high drop-out **(4)** ....., especially on the rally's difficult first **(5)** ..... across central China and over the high mountain **(6)** ..... of the Himalayas. 'If twenty-five cars **(7)** ..... it to Paris, we'll be doing well,' he says.

The first Beijing-Paris car rally took place in 1907. It was won by Prince Borghese, an Italian adventurer, who crossed the **(8)** ..... line just a few metres **(9)** ..... of the only other car to complete the race. At the time his achievement was **(10)** ..... as comparable to that of the great explorer, Marco Polo.

According to the rules, all the cars in the rally must be more than thirty years old, which means that the rough roads and high altitude are a **(11)** ..... test of both the cars and the drivers. A sense of adventure is essential. One driver said, 'Our **(12)** ..... is to have a good time, enjoy the experience and the magnificent scenery – and the adventure of a lifetime.'

1   **A**   adapt   **B**   moderate   **C**   improve   **D**   form

2   **A**   head   **B**   move   **C**   set   **D**   try

3   **A**   vision   **B**   fantasy   **C**   hope   **D**   dream

4   **A**   rate   **B**   number   **C**   speed   **D**   frequency

5   **A**   period   **B**   stage   **C**   time   **D**   round

6   **A**   crossings   **B**   passes   **C**   directions   **D**   passages

7   **A**   get   **B**   take   **C**   have   **D**   make

8   **A**   closing   **B**   final   **C**   ending   **D**   finishing

9   **A**   forward   **B**   ahead   **C**   front   **D**   advance

10 **A**   thought   **B**   referred   **C**   regarded   **D**   noted

11 **A**   firm   **B**   strict   **C**   severe   **D**   grave

12 **A**   aim   **B**   target   **C**   proposal   **D**   intent

Part 2

For questions **13–27**, read the text below and think of the word which best fits each gap. Use only **one** word in each gap. There is an example at the beginning (**0**).

Write your answers **IN CAPITAL LETTERS on the separate answer sheet**.

Example:

0	T	O																

Central Park

If you have the chance **(0)** ..... take a walk through Central Park in New York, you will get a quick tour of the wide range of cultures and people who live in the city. **(13)** ..... man speeds along on a racing bike singing **(14)** ..... the top of his voice, **(15)** ..... dances to the beat of techno music coming from a tape recorder.

Central Park, the first public park built in America, allows for just about **(16)** ..... conceivable leisure activity in a rectangle of just over one and a half square kilometres. But it may **(17)** ..... that its best use is for the most entertaining sport in New York – people watching. Visitors can have **(18)** ..... better introduction to the diversity of New York than a stroll in this park.

Central Park did not always embrace **(19)** ..... a variety of human life. Having won a competition for the park's design in 1858, Frederick Law Olmsted and Calvert Vaux envisaged the place **(20)** ..... an oasis of calm in a disorderly city. The idea **(21)** ..... to create a place where the upper-class citizens of the city could take gentle exercise **(22)** ..... being disturbed. However, the park authorities never managed to enforce a regime of order. Olmsted **(23)** ..... been determined to create the illusion of the countryside in the heart of New York. The fact that skyscrapers are now visible **(24)** ..... the tops of the park's tallest trees **(25)** ...... certainly have horrified him. But this contrast between country and city landscape is **(26)** ..... gives the park **(27)** ..... very own special charm.

Part 3

For questions **28–37**, read the text below. Use the word given in capitals at the end of some of the lines to form a word that fits in the gap **in the same line**. There is an example at the beginning **(0)**.

Write your answers **IN CAPITAL LETTERS on the separate answer sheet**.

Example:

0	R	E	V	O	L	U	T	I	O	N	A	R	Y						

Why new technology sometimes fails

In recent decades, many inventors have come up with **(0)** ..... new   **REVOLUTION**
products that have promised to change the way we live. Some, like
mobile phones and laptop computers, have certainly done that, but the
majority have completely failed to live up to everybody's **(28)** ..... and have   **EXPECT**
quickly been forgotten. So what went wrong? **(29)** ....., there are four tests   **BASIC**
that any new invention must pass to ensure its **(30)** ..... .   **SURVIVE**

First of all, is there sufficient consumer demand? If nobody wants the
product, then no matter how brilliant the idea behind it, it's not going to
take off. Secondly, commercial **(31)** ..... is always very much related to   **SUCCEED**
how **(32)** ..... the product is. The costlier it is initially, the less likely it is to   **AFFORD**
become a big seller, **(33)** ..... of how interesting and desirable it might   **REGARD**
seem.

(34) ..... is another important element. After all, if a product is so complex   **SIMPLE**
that non-technical salespeople are **(35)** ..... of explaining how it works and   **CAPABLE**
what it can do for potential customers, then it will be hard to sell.

Finally, any new gadget or domestic appliance needs to be both reliable
and **(36)** ..... . If it doesn't do what the salesperson claims, and do so   **EFFECT**
(37) ..... over a period of time for its users, then word will soon get round   **REPEAT**
and nobody else will buy it.

Part 4

For questions **38–42**, think of **one** word only which can be used appropriately in all three sentences. Here is an example (**0**).

Example:

0 The committee decided to .... the money equally between the two charities.

I can't believe that John and Maggie have decided to .... up after 20 years of marriage.

To serve a watermelon you need to .... it down the centre with a sharp knife.

Example:

0	S	P	L	I	T													

Write **only** the missing word **IN CAPITAL LETTERS on the separate answer sheet**.

---

38 Mrs Loreno .... me a copy of the book she had written many years ago.

The results of the survey .... that people are eating more healthily than five years ago.

Petra .... no interest in science when she was at school.

39 You might as well do your homework now; you'll have to do it at some ....

The problem with our Geography teacher is that it takes him half an hour to get to the .... of the lesson.

Don't get upset by what Carlo says; politeness isn't really his strong ....

40 The government needs to .... major financial and political decisions in the coming year.

It doesn't .... much intelligence to realise that the plan to ban parking in the city centre won't work.

I don't think we really have much choice at this stage – all we can do is .... our accountant's advice.

41 The tutor said the organisation of ideas in my essay was .... , but I needed to do more work on the conclusion.

They say that the secret of a .... skin is drinking plenty of liquids and eating lots of fruit and vegetables.

It was a long time before the road was .... of traffic, so that she could overtake the lorry.

42 The band got its first big .... in 2003 when it played in America.

It's rained hard for two days and our trip won't go ahead unless there's a .... in the weather.

Sam and Anna went to Spain for a short .... in September.

Part 5

For questions **43–50**, complete the second sentence so that it has a similar meaning to the first sentence, using the word given. **Do not change the word given.** You must use between **three** and **six** words, including the word given. Here is an example (**0**).

Example:

0 Fernanda refused to wear her sister's old dress.

NOT

Fernanda said that .... her sister's old dress.

The gap can be filled with the words 'she would not wear', so you write:

Example: | **0** | SHE WOULD NOT WEAR |

Write the missing words **IN CAPITAL LETTERS on the separate answer sheet**.

---

43 The reduction in the price of the magazines led to a growth in sales.

RESULT

Sales of the magazine .... the reduction in the price.

44 I think the weather will improve next week.

CHANGE

I think there'll be .... better in the weather next week.

45 Phoebe was surprised to be offered a place on the course.

CAME

The offer of a place on the course .... Phoebe.

46 If he doesn't get that job, who knows what he'll do!

KNOWING

If he doesn't get that job, ... what he'll do!

47 'Do you want to go and see the new play at the Arts Centre?' Petra asked her friend.

INTERESTED

Petra asked her friend whether .... to see the new play at the Arts Centre.

48 Georgia hasn't written to me recently.

HEARD

I .... a while.

49 They put Roger in charge of health and safety at the factory.

MADE

Roger .... for health and safety in the factory.

50 It is important to be well prepared for an interview because if you make a mistake, you may not get the job.

COST

A mistake in an interview may .... so it is important to be well prepared.

PAPER 4   LISTENING (approximately 40 minutes)

Part 1

You will hear three different extracts. For questions **1–6**, choose the answer (**A**, **B** or **C**) which fits best according to what you hear. There are two questions for each extract.

Extract One

You hear part of a radio discussion about the ongoing television dramas known as soap operas.

1   The man says that soap operas now feature more dramatic events because

    A   they have to appear similar to imported series.

    B   the audience has requested more exciting storylines.

    C   this can help to generate higher levels of media publicity.

2   The two speakers agree that soaps should not

    A   include social questions in their stories.

    B   tell their audiences what they ought to do.

    C   encourage discussion of difficult topics.

Extract Two

You overhear a conversation in a shop between a jewellery-maker and a customer.

3   The jeweller took up her craft because

    A   she was unable to continue in her original career.

    B   she was persuaded to do so by fellow students.

    C   she found it less challenging than drawing.

4   When asked about her attitude to her craft, the jeweller reveals

    A   the optimism which stimulates her best work.

    B   satisfaction that her income has increased.

    C   confidence in the popularity of her style.

Extract Three

You overhear two colleagues, Richard and Kate, discussing a round-the-world trip Kate is planning to go on.

5   When talking to Kate about her trip, Richard is

    A   giving her some advice.

    B   seeking to clarify her objectives.

    C   warning her of unexpected problems.

6   When asked about her fellow travellers, Kate reveals

    A   her level of respect for them.

    B   her degree of dependence on them.

    C   her feelings of affection towards them.

Part 2

You will hear part of a radio programme in which an expert on theatre history is talking about the life of a famous actress called Helen Perry. For questions **7–14**, complete the sentences.

Helen Perry

The common view that acting was an unsuitable career

for a woman was shared by [_____ **7**]

Helen admitted that her greatest problems in acting involved [_____ **8**]

In her fifties, Helen had to have a dangerous

[_____ **9**] which saved her career.

Helen's broad popularity reflects her skill as both a

[_____ **10**] and a classical actress.

Helen was so popular that a brand of [_____ **11**] was named after her.

Evidence of Helen's skill as a writer can be found in some of the

[_____ **12**] that she wrote.

We can get an idea of the quality of her later performances from

[_____ **13**] of the time.

What pleased Helen most was the attention she received from

[_____ **14**]

Part 3

You will hear a radio interview with the writer, Tom Davies. For questions **15–20**, choose the answer (**A**, **B**, **C** or **D**) which fits best according to what you hear.

15 How does Tom feel now about being a writer?

    A It is no longer as exciting as it was.
    B He used to get more pleasure from it.
    C He is still surprised when it goes well.
    D It is less difficult to do these days.

16 How does Tom feel about the idea for a novel before he begins writing it?

    A He lacks confidence in himself.
    B He is very secretive about it.
    C He likes to get reactions to it.
    D He is uncertain how it will develop.

17 Tom's behaviour when beginning a new novel can best be described as

    A determined.
    B enthusiastic.
    C impulsive.
    D unpredictable.

18 What does Tom say happens to writers as they get older and better known?

    A Their friends are more honest with them.
    B Publishers are less likely to criticise them.
    C They get less objective about their own work.
    D They find it harder to accept criticism.

19 What does Tom admit about his novels?

    A They are not completely imaginary.
    B They are open to various interpretations.
    C They do not reflect his personal views.
    D They do not make very good films.

20 What did Tom feel about the first film he was involved in making?

    A He enjoyed being part of a team.
    B He found it much too stressful.
    C He earned too little money from it.
    D He was reassured by how easy it was.

Part 4

You will hear five short extracts in which people are reading from their autobiographies.

TASK ONE

For questions **21–25**, choose from the list **A–H** what each speaker is saying.

TASK TWO

For questions **26–30**, choose from the list **A–H** the feeling each speaker expresses.

While you listen you must complete both tasks.

A I made up my mind about something.	**A** regret
B I had a piece of luck.	**B** relief
C My popularity started to decline.	**C** annoyance
D I received some bad publicity.	**D** optimism
E I achieved an ambition.	**E** anxiety
F My attitude to fame changed.	**F** embarrassment
G I made a mistake.	**G** indifference
H I turned down an opportunity.	**H** disappointment

Speaker 1	21		Speaker 1	26
Speaker 2	22		Speaker 2	27
Speaker 3	23		Speaker 3	28
Speaker 4	24		Speaker 4	29
Speaker 5	25		Speaker 5	30

Visual materials for the Speaking test

- How might the people be feeling?
- What part might music play in their lives?

- How might the people be feeling?
- Why might moments like these be necessary in their lives?

- How difficult might it be for these people to make their hopes and dreams come true?
- Which two are most likely to become reality?

- How difficult might it have been for these people to acquire their skills?
- What might have motivated them to aim for perfection?

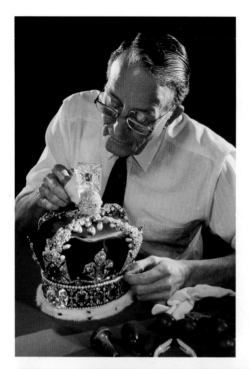

- Why might the people be saying goodbye?
- How might they be feeling?

- How successful would these pictures be in encouraging city people to take more exercise?
- Which two pictures should be included in the leaflet?

- Why might the people be measuring these things?
- How important is it for them to be accurate?

- What makes people want to explore?
- What risks might they be taking?

- Why do people find these issues worrying?
- In which two cases are improvements most needed?

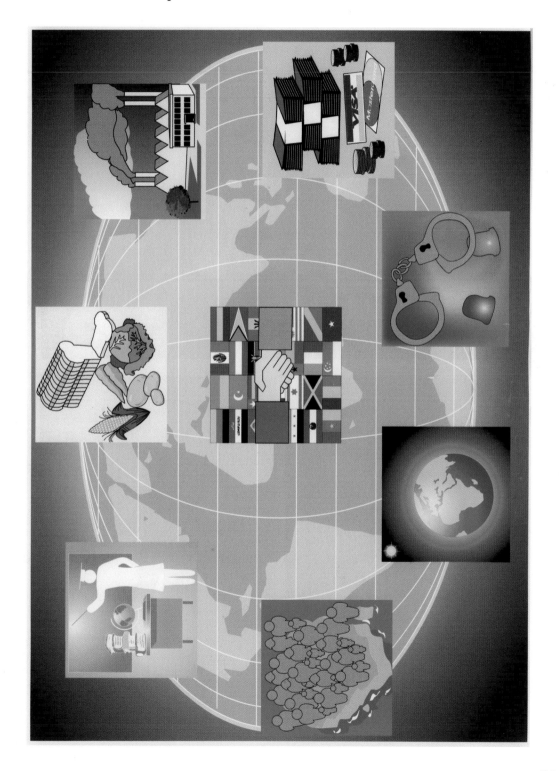

- Why might the people be feeling happy?
- How memorable might these occasions be?

- Why might the people have chosen to do these activities together?
- What skills do they need?

- What skills might people need to do these different jobs?
- Which job would be the most, and which the least, challenging?

PAPER 5   SPEAKING (15 minutes)

There are two examiners. One (the interlocutor) conducts the test, providing you with the necessary materials and explaining what you have to do. The other examiner (the assessor) is introduced to you, but then takes no further part in the interaction.

Part 1 (3 minutes)

The interlocutor first asks you and your partner a few questions. The interlocutor asks candidates for some information about themselves, then widens the scope of the questions by asking about, e.g. candidates' leisure activities, studies, travel and daily life. Candidates are expected to respond to the interlocutor's questions, and listen to what their partner has to say.

Part 2 (a one-minute long turn for each candidate, plus 30-second response from the second candidate)

You are each given the opportunity to talk for about a minute, and to comment briefly after your partner has spoken.

The interlocutor gives you a set of pictures and asks you to talk about them for about one minute. It is important to listen carefully to the interlocutor's instructions. The interlocutor then asks your partner a question about your pictures and your partner responds briefly.

You are then given another set of pictures to look at. Your partner talks about these pictures for about one minute. This time the interlocutor asks you a question about your partner's pictures and you respond briefly.

Part 3 (approximately 4 minutes)

In this part of the test you and your partner are asked to talk together. The interlocutor places a new set of pictures on the table between you. This stimulus provides the basis for a discussion.

The interlocutor explains what you have to do.

Part 4 (approximately 4 minutes)

The interlocutor asks some further questions, which leads to a more general discussion of what you have talked about in Part 3. You may comment on your partner's answers if you wish.

Test 3

PAPER 1   READING (1 hour 15 minutes)

Part 1

You are going to read three extracts which are all concerned in some way with entertainment. For questions **1–6**, choose the answer (**A**, **B**, **C** or **D**) which you think fits best according to the text. Mark your answers **on the separate answer sheet**.

An Actor's Life Story

Me: Stories of My Life is Katharine Hepburn's account of her upbringing, her long career in film and theater, and her intriguing private life. This autobiography is a pleasure to read because it's punchy, courageous, and intimate. She begins her story with the history of her close-knit, progressive family and goes through her school days – acting in the school plays and getting suspended. Her description of her early career in theater is fascinating, as she was fired by nearly every person who employed her. She was 'very young and absolutely outrageous and full of a sort of wild confidence based on nothing but energy and ego'. Audiences had mixed responses. Ironically, male producers were the ones to fire her, and their wives always chastized them, saying that someday she was going to be a big star.

At least, that's how Hepburn puts it. She details both her triumphs and failures, and she manages a charming combination of rampant self-worship and witty humility, but there's no objectivity here. And that makes it all the better. Her descriptions of her life and work are anecdotal – stories from the set, and details about which producers treated her well and which badly. She is a great storyteller and indulges our curiosity without compromising her integrity. Her autobiography deals with several layers, including her relationship with 'that creature whom I created', her onscreen alter ego. It's a fascinating look at a spirited misfit's rise to fame, as much a cultural study of the entertainment industry as it is a personal psychological journey.

1   Why does the reviewer find Katharine Hepburn's early acting career interesting?

    A   Producers recognised that she had star quality.
    B   Audiences disapproved of her acting style.
    C   She often lost jobs in the theatre.
    D   She had more self-confidence than older actors.

2   What does the reviewer suggest when he writes: 'At least, that's how Hepburn puts it.' in line 9?

    A   She is a very good storyteller.
    B   Her style of writing is very exciting.
    C   Her account is one-sided.
    D   She uses the book to criticise producers.

Glastonbury

Film director Julien Temple's career has contained more ups and downs than a day at a theme park, but things are most definitely in the ascendancy with *Glastonbury*. A magical documentary recounting the 35 tumultuous years of the Glastonbury Music Festival, this is an exhilarating experience – I would say, nearly as good as being at the festival itself. Drawing upon 900 hours of footage submitted by the public, 450 hours shot by Temple himself, broadcast concert material and archival news coverage, *Glastonbury* is a sprawling affair that succeeds because it captures the spirit of the festival itself: rough rather than polished; organic rather than manufactured.

For the most part Temple tells his story chronologically, tracing the festival's roots as a hippie gathering in the 1970s, through a politically active period in the early 1980s, and an involvement with alternative lifestyles in the late 1980s. It is noteworthy that, as the event becomes less about counter-culture and more about product placement, the documentary's predominant background noise becomes mobile ringtones. As well as providing a fascinating social snapshot of festival goers, *Glastonbury* is also a celebration of the hundreds of bands who've played the festival over the years. Temple does not make the mistake of overloading the film with music, and selects his acts carefully. Most represent particularly memorable moments in the festival's history, in particular Pulp's storming rendition of *Common People* in the 1990s. Put simply, *Glastonbury* rocks.

3   The writer particularly enjoyed *Glastonbury* because the film

   A   has been skilfully edited.
   B   reflects the character of its subject.
   C   is made by a director he admires.
   D   contains footage he has not seen before.

4   What significant change in the festival is highlighted by the film?

   A   The audiences are much larger than in the past.
   B   An increasing number of bands are playing each year.
   C   The festival attracts more celebrity bands than previously.
   D   The festival is run along more commercial lines these days.

Writing for the Stage

A playwright creates scripts and tells stories through the words and actions of characters. While the output of the playwright can stand on its own as literature, its potential is fully realised only when the skills of all the other theatre artists combine to transform the script into a production of a play.

A playwright's tool kit needs to contain:

- a vivid imagination
- a gripping story to tell
- insight into what makes people tick
- a good ear for capturing authentic dialogue
- working knowledge of the elements of dramatic structure
- an understanding of theatre's non-verbal means of expression – sound, movement, setting, costume, lighting, music, pacing and stage picture.

Playwrights sometimes bring actors and directors into the task of script creation in a valuable process known as collective creation. Here everyone takes a hand in researching the narrative and developing the script. But because the skilful ordering and re-creation of events is central to the playwright's art, the final task of shaping the raw material into a coherent playscript is normally the playwright's responsibility. Playwrights may also develop a new script with guidance from a dramaturg, who is a kind of editor. A dramaturg's feedback on a new script may be given at any point in the process, from the first draft through to rehearsals. One way of doing this is through workshops, organised by the dramaturg, which involve a reading or scene study of the script by a director and professional actors. A new script is often strengthened by the feedback the playwright receives through this process.

5   What is the writer's main purpose in this text?

    A   to outline the difficulties of writing plays
    B   to describe what a playwright's job involves
    C   to persuade people to write for the theatre
    D   to distinguish between actors and playwrights

6   In the writer's opinion, a theatrical script

    A   often depends for its success on the approval of a dramaturg.
    B   will lose some of its impact during the production process.
    C   can usefully be created by a group of people.
    D   is rarely as highly regarded as a piece of literature.

Part 2

You are going to read an extract from a magazine article about psychology. Six paragraphs have been removed from the extract. Choose from the paragraphs **A–G** the one which fits each gap (**7–12**). There is one extra paragraph which you do not need to use. Mark your answers **on the separate answer sheet**.

Human Behaviour

Peter Jones reports on how groups function.

Unless you're a loner, you're probably a member of many different groups. Some are long lasting, like your family, while others, such as a football crowd, are temporary. Every group functions in different ways but there are still some common psychological features to any group.

7

Being part of a group changes the way you behave. The presence of others has a generally arousing effect on the nervous system. This is natural – you don't know what they will do. They may move about, speak to you, or even attack you, and your brain has to pay attention to all these messages. Having others around is just distracting. It divides your attention, so you can't focus on the task in hand.

8

But when it comes to complex tasks, the prospect of not being evaluated may free you from anxiety, so encouraging you to perform better. To test this, psychologists asked volunteers to carry out a complex computer task in separate rooms. Some were told performance would be evaluated individually – causing performance anxiety – while others were told the results would be averaged with the rest of the group. As expected, the second group did better than the first.

9

The problem becomes even worse when individuals are disguised with war paint or uniforms. Analysis shows that the more people there are in a mob, the greater the antisocial behaviour. Being 'submerged' within a group

does have many negative connotations but it's not always a bad thing. Instead of thinking about a rowdy mob, think of relaxing, dancing and enjoying yourself at a party where you are also just a part of the crowd.

10

But surprisingly, research has shown that the use of this technique by groups isn't that effective in either the number or quality of ideas generated. You get better results if you set people to work individually on a problem. We also tend to assume that decisions made by groups are better than those made by individuals, which is why we form committees.

11

But any group can get a decision badly wrong, because their thought processes can go awry. This is a process psychologists call 'groupthink'. A close-knit group of advisers isolated from argument and criticism can grow to believe they can do no wrong. The group then becomes more important than the individuals who are part of it. Further, a leadership style which concentrates on the group rather than the individual can contribute to this.

12

Many, but not all, leaders show dominance in the group. But the dominant person in the group doesn't always make the best leader, and it isn't necessarily true that having the smartest people always makes for the most successful group.

A This lack of individual accountability may lead to people letting go of their inhibitions – a process known as 'deindividuation'. Sometimes this is dangerous, releasing violent and impulsive behaviours that individuals would never dream of indulging in alone.

B They have a need for power, characterised by talking a lot, wanting to be listened to and to make decisions. In a group it can be easy to spot the dominant people. They make eye contact, point and even touch people but don't encourage return gestures. Such behaviour studies have been key in shaping business organisation.

C For example, in general, humans are social animals, that's why we get together in groups in the first place. Important elements of our individual identity come from being part of a group. Most people enjoy being in a group – it's a way of forming emotionally satisfying relationships.

D But it has to be a carefully selected team, not a randomly generated group, if creative decisions are to be made. In fact, theory on team building has shown that it is better if people work in small teams of complementary pairs. Big teams don't get anything done, even though people like them.

E For a group and its behaviour are shaped by who is in charge and the roles the other members play. A good front man or woman is persuasive, not directive, communicates and speaks clearly, listens well and appeals to group members' emotions and feelings as well as thoughts and ideas.

F So, how does all this stimulation affect achievement? It has been argued that people do better on simple well-rehearsed activities when they're with others than when they are alone. Also, if their individual efforts within the group are not being monitored, there's a tendency to relax and merge into the crowd.

G Another positive feature of groups is that they generate ideas and opinions, and use these to make decisions. That's why the modern trend in teaching is for students to work in small groups to prepare presentations and why brainstorming is so popular in the work context.

Part 3

You are going to read a magazine article about an ancient Greek shipwreck. For questions **13–19**, choose the answer (**A**, **B**, **C** or **D**) which you think fits best according to the text. Mark your answers **on the separate answer sheet**.

Discovering the secrets of an ancient Greek shipwreck
John Green reports on a recent find in the Mediterranean.

While other members of my team explored the wreck of a small Greek merchant ship that sank off the Turkish coast more than 2,400 years ago, I hovered above them in a submersible. One diver, an archaeologist, placed an amphora, or two-handled jar, inside a lifting basket. Another vacuumed sediment from the site by fanning sand into the mouth of a nearly vertical suction pipe. Two more were taking measurements, carefully, but of necessity quickly, for at this depth each diver had only 20 minutes to complete the morning's assigned task. Any longer, and they would require lengthy decompression, to avoid the divers' ailment known as the bends.

In four decades of diving on shipwrecks, I'd been too engrossed in carrying out similar tasks to think of the families whose loved ones may have disappeared long ago. I had always concentrated on the technical features of my trade. I had stopped diving regularly 15 years before this exploration, turning over the bulk of the underwater work to a younger generation, but I continue to make inspection dives on most wrecks we excavate.

line 10   This was not just any wreck. Although I've been involved in uncovering the remains of much older ships, and of more than a hundred ancient shipwrecks along the Turkish coast, I had never even seen a wreck from the fifth century BC. Preliminary photographs of the cargo dated it to the third quarter of the century, during the Golden Age of classical Greece. Was there any other time when architecture, philosophy, sculpture, drama and politics reached near perfection in so few years? Athens, then as now the major city in Greece, controlled an empire stretching from one side of the Aegean Sea to the other. None of this would have been possible without naval might and maritime commerce. Athens could not even feed its own people without the grain imported by sea.

Back in the present, I brought the submersible up to the surface and returned to our camp, a summer home for our team of upwards of 30 people. Construction had been a major challenge. While looking for a suitable location I had struggled on that cape, which centuries of rough seas have eroded into sharp teeth of solid rock, but the long-term advantage of quartering in optimum proximity to the exploration site outweighed the short-term disadvantage of spending two months transforming the inhospitable rock into a comfortable camp.

During our three-year exploration of the wreck we excavated examples of nearly every type of jar that the classical Greeks made for wine or water. Many types – particularly the cheaper ones – might have been used as tableware by the ship's crew, but they were far in excess of what would have been required. We concluded therefore that they must have been cargo. Almost all seem to have been manufactured on the island of Chios, close to where the ship sank. We also discovered in the seabed two marble discs, which we guessed were the ship's eyes. It has long been known from vase paintings that classical Greek ships – like those from other cultures – had eyes to give them life or help them see their way through the waves. Although warships were known to have had naturalistic marble eyes attached to them, most scholars assumed that the eyes on more modest merchant ships were depicted as simple circles painted onto the sides of the vessel. Our marble eyes, the first from an actual ancient wreck and the first associated with a merchant ship, suggest otherwise. Not only were they made of marble, they had, like those of warships, been painted to show both the pupil and the iris.

Did the sailors who depended on these eyes for safety survive the ship's last voyage? They could have lived through the actual sinking. The ship was less than a hundred yards from land when it sank, so they might have swum towards the shore. And we know from Greek literature that some ships had lifeboats. But proximity to land and having lifeboats are no guarantees of safety. Even if some had swum to shore, it's hard to imagine that many managed to crawl up on the exposed and sharp rocks while being smashed by waves like those that almost certainly sank their ship.

Several of our finds are important in the history of shipbuilding. The cargo, though, was not of great significance. There were the ceramic jars, most of them probably made along the coast where we were diving. A few came from north eastern Greece and were carrying a kind of pine tar used for purposes as varied as making wooden ships watertight and flavouring wine. The nature of the cargo suggests why the tools, weights, coins and personal possessions we usually find on ancient wrecks were absent: perhaps the ship made only day trips between Chios and nearby islands.

13 In the first paragraph, what point does the writer make about the exploration?

  A It was most effective when carried out by a small team.
  B It required each diver to possess a variety of skills.
  C It had to take into account risks to the divers.
  D It had been made easier by technological developments.

14 What does the writer suggest about himself in the second paragraph?

  A He had developed every skill that was needed for exploring wrecks.
  B He had benefited by changing his role in explorations.
  C He was pleased he had started training younger divers.
  D He was aware he distanced himself from aspects of his work.

15 The writer uses the words 'not just any wreck' in line 10 to imply that

  A he had been searching for the ship for a considerable time.
  B this was not the only ship found off the coast of Turkey.
  C finding this particular ship was of exceptional significance.
  D the ship was in better condition than most wrecks.

16 What was the writer's priority for the camp?

  A how comfortable it could be made
  B how quickly it could be constructed
  C how near it was to the wreck
  D how much land was available

17 The writer decided on the purpose of the jars on the basis that

  A they were too valuable to be used on board ship.
  B there was a larger quantity of them than the crew needed.
  C there were more different types than the crew needed.
  D they were manufactured in Chios.

18 What was significant about the ship's eyes that were found?

  A It had been thought that eyes like these were only used on warships.
  B They were different from the eyes on ships in vase paintings.
  C It was unusual for eyes to be placed in this position on a ship.
  D They were surprisingly similar to eyes on ships from other cultures.

19 What is the writer's opinion about the chances of the sailors having survived?

  A They would have been too far from land to swim ashore.
  B They would have found it difficult to climb onto land.
  C The sea would have been too rough to swim in.
  D Their lifeboats would have been destroyed by the waves.

Part 4

You are going to read an article in which scientists and writers nominate their favourite science fiction authors. For questions **20–34**, choose from the authors (**A–D**). The authors may be chosen more than once.

Mark your answers **on the separate answer sheet**.

Which science fiction author

has an unusually broad readership?	20
put a high value on the process of thinking up original ideas?	21
predicted some disturbing aspects of modern society?	22
lacked a sense of style when it came to writing?	23
was very careful in the way he presented scientific matters?	24
used science principally to generate interesting situations for human characters?	25
was equally renowned in other professional fields?	26
made disasters appear likely and even imminent?	27
promoted public interest in scientific issues?	28
brought new life to an existing literary style?	29
owes most of his literary reputation to one particular work?	30
skilfully describes reactions to developments in the field of science?	31
departed from the conventional settings of science fiction stories?	32
dealt with themes which some people have failed to recognise?	33
proposed a theory which took time to gain acceptance?	34

FAVOURITE SCIENCE FICTION AUTHORS

Top scientists and writers nominate their favourite science fiction authors

A Isaac Asimov

Isaac Asimov, the founding father of modern science fiction, came out as a clear favourite among today's scientists and writers. Trained as a chemist, Asimov also held a teaching post at Boston University for many years. 'Although not as elegant a prose writer as many of his contemporaries, Asimov was, however, very rigorous scientifically, and thoughtful about how he projected scientific ideas into the future,' says Philip Ball, a writer of popular science books. Two works mark Asimov out as the master of the genre: *I, Robot*, and the *Foundation* trilogy. In the *Foundation* series, science and maths were used to predict and plan the development of societies, something which Mark Brake, professor of science communication, thinks may be a touch farfetched: 'We often can't even predict a flood in a nearby town, let alone how a society behaves a thousand years in the future. Unlike a lot of sci-fi writers, Asimov knew how to explain the science, and was a keen populariser of real science,' says Brake. 'But what sets him apart is that he was also masterful at documenting human responses to scientific progress.'

B John Wyndham

John Wyndham, author of *The Day of the Triffids* and many other extremely successful works, was one of the few science fiction writers to become hugely popular with people who never normally read science fiction. Julia Higgins, professor of polymer science, describes Wyndham's writing as 'good novels in which there were real people, and the science issues simply pushed the real people into dramatic circumstances.' Up until the late 1940s, sci-fi was almost exclusively set in space, and involved what Wyndham himself described as 'the adventures of galactic gangsters'. Wyndham's deliberate choice of innocuously 'cosy' English backdrops is central to the power of his novels, implying that apocalypse could occur at any time – or, indeed, be happening in the next village at this moment. Although Wyndham did not invent the English catastrophe novel, he re-established the genre and examined its themes with the freshness of a pioneer.

C Fred Hoyle

One of Britain's most creative scientists, Hoyle was as well known for his far-reaching work in the 1950s and 60s as a mathematician and astrophysicist as he was as a science fiction author. Hoyle felt that his science fiction writing was an important complement to his scientific career, and was convinced that major discoveries were most likely to come from an exercise of the creative imagination. He originated the notion that life arrived on earth by way of an asteroid striking the planet, a hypothesis which, although ridiculed at the time, has now earned respectable scientific credentials.

Hoyle wrote and co-authored a number of highly-regarded works including *A for Andromeda: A Novel for Tomorrow* (1962), and *Ossian's Ride* (1959). But it is his first novel, *The Black Cloud* (1957), for which he is chiefly renowned as a sci-fi writer. Evolutionary biologist Richard Dawkins sees it as a major influential work: 'In *The Black Cloud* I learned about scientific method and information theory – the interchangeability of different kinds of information.' In the novel, humans try to communicate with an alien intelligence, in the form of a cloud of gas, by playing it piano music translated into radio signals. 'Today we see information theory in genetic code and the translation of information from one computer to another,' says Dawkins.

D Philip K Dick

Philip K Dick is certainly one of the most adapted science fiction novelists: his 1968 novel *Do Androids Dream of Electric Sheep?* became the seminal film *Blade Runner*; *We Can Remember It For You Wholesale* became the movie *Total Recall* and *Minority Report* was filmed by Steven Spielberg in 2002. But his cerebral works were underrated for years until *Blade Runner* brought acclaim – only months after his death. 'The fact that what Dick is entertaining us about is sanity and madness, time and death, sin and salvation, has escaped most critics,' says writer Ursula K Le Guin.

'Most of Dick's books are concerned with the question of how we know what is real. These are the key questions for all of us who study the neural aspects of consciousness,' says Chris Frith of University College London's Institute of Cognitive Neuroscience. Dick's writing dealt with unsettling ideas such as the theft of memory and personality, and with what he saw as the false realities manufactured by the media, governments, and big corporations. Writer Robin McKie admires the remarkable foresight in Dick's works: 'Nowadays, when identities are stolen along with mobile phones and credit cards, when CCTVs scan our movements, and when the news is constantly being manipulated, Dick looks like an inspirational visionary.'

PAPER 2 WRITING (1 hour 30 minutes)

Part 1

You **must** answer this question. Write your answer in **180–220** words in an appropriate style.

---

1   You have returned from a holiday in Britain which combined sightseeing with language classes. You have been asked to write a report about it for the Head of the English Department at your college.

Read the advertisement for the holiday and an extract from your diary below. Then, **using the information appropriately**, write a report for the Head of the English Department explaining what you thought about the holiday and saying whether or not you would recommend it to others, and why.

GET TO KNOW BRITAIN

**Coach trips to famous towns
Varied programme of activities
Language tuition
First class hotel accommodation**

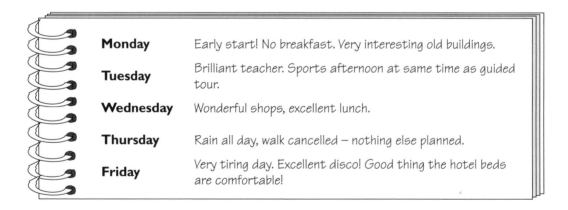

Monday	Early start! No breakfast. Very interesting old buildings.
Tuesday	Brilliant teacher. Sports afternoon at same time as guided tour.
Wednesday	Wonderful shops, excellent lunch.
Thursday	Rain all day, walk cancelled – nothing else planned.
Friday	Very tiring day. Excellent disco! Good thing the hotel beds are comfortable!

Write your **report**. You should use your own words as far as possible.

Part 2

Choose **one** of the following writing tasks. Your answer should follow exactly the instructions given. Write approximately **220–260** words.

---

2   You see this announcement in an international student magazine.

> ### Youth Matters
> We are preparing a special edition of our magazine dedicated to the problems that affect young people in different countries today, in particular, those relating to work, education, or the environment. Write us an article about the most important aspects of **one** of these issues facing young people today in **your** country.

Write your **article**.

3   A friend of your family is applying for a job with a travel company as a tourist guide for English speaking tourists visiting your country. The company has asked you to provide a character reference for your friend.

The reference should indicate how long you have known the person. It must also include a detailed description of the person's character and the reasons why he or she would be suitable for the job.

Write your **reference**.

4
> ### COMPETITION
> We will build a leisure facility if you can convince us about what you need – it may be an art gallery, a sports centre or a multi-screen cinema . . . .
> Write to us and tell us about **one** leisure facility you would like to have.
>
> Enter our competition and tell us:
> * what leisure facility you would like and why you think it is needed
> * what you would like the leisure facility to provide
> * which groups of people in your community would most benefit from this facility.

Write your **competition entry**.

5   Answer **one** of the following two questions based on **one** of the titles below.

(a) Adriana Trigiani: *Big Stone Gap*
Your teacher has asked you to write an essay about *Big Stone Gap*. Your essay should discuss two different relationships between parents and children in *Big Stone Gap*. You should comment on the strengths and weaknesses of these relationships and should suggest how each of these relationships could have been improved.

Write your **essay**.

(b) Dick Francis: *In the Frame*
You decide to write a review of *In the Frame* for a web site. Your review should focus on the book as a thriller. To what extent do you think most people would find it deserves to be called a thriller? Explain which scene you personally found the most exciting.

Write your **review**.

PAPER 3   USE OF ENGLISH (1 hour)

Part 1

For questions **1–12**, read the text below and then decide which answer (**A, B, C** or **D**) best fits each gap. There is an example at the beginning (**0**).

Mark your answers **on the separate answer sheet**.

Example:

0 A adjust   **B** fit   **C** reform   **D** move

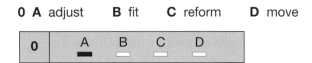

Smart shoes

Smart shoes that **(0)** ..... their size throughout the day could soon be available. A prototype has already been produced and a commercial **(1)** ..... may be in production within a few years. The shoe contains sensors that constantly check the amount of **(2)** ..... left in it. If the foot has become too large, a tiny valve opens and the shoe **(3)** ..... slightly. The entire control system is about 5mm square and is located inside the shoe. This radical shoe **(4)** ..... a need because the volume of the **(5)** ..... foot can change by as much as 8% during the course of the day. The system is able to learn about the wearer's feet and **(6)** ..... up a picture of the size of his or her feet throughout the day. It will allow the shoes to change in size by up to 8% so that they always fit **(7)** ..... . They are obviously more comfortable and less likely to **(8)** ..... blisters. From an athlete's point of view, they can help improve **(9)** ..... a little, and that is why the first **(10)** ..... for the system is likely to be in a sports shoe.

Eventually, this system will find a **(11)** ..... in many other household items, from beds that automatically change to fit the person sleeping in them, to power tools that **(12)** ..... themselves to the user's hand for better grip.

---

1   **A**   assortment   **B**   version   **C**   style   **D**   variety

2   **A**   room   **B**   gap   **C**   area   **D**   emptiness

3   **A**   amplifies   **B**   develops   **C**   expands   **D**   increases

4   **A**   detects   **B**   finds   **C**   meets   **D**   faces

5   **A**   average   **B**   general   **C**   usual   **D**   medium

6   **A**   build   **B**   pick   **C**   grow   **D**   set

7   **A**   exactly   **B**   absolutely   **C**   completely   **D**   totally

8   **A**   provoke   **B**   form   **C**   initiate   **D**   cause

9   **A**   achievement   **B**   performance   **C**   success   **D**   winning

10 **A**   purpose   **B**   exercise   **C**   use   **D**   operation

11 **A**   function   **B**   part   **C**   way   **D**   place

12 **A**   shape   **B**   change   **C**   respond   **D**   convert

Part 2

For questions **13–27**, read the article below and think of the word which best fits each gap. Use only **one** word in each gap. There is an example at the beginning (**0**).

Write your answers **IN CAPITAL LETTERS on the separate answer sheet**.

Example: | **0** | B | E | E | N | | | | | | | | | | | | | | | |

Blue whales

Blue whales, the world's largest animals, have **(0)** ..... sighted again in British waters for the first time in **(13)** ..... least twenty years. Indications that a population of blue whales was inhabiting the waters west **(14)** ..... Scotland came for the first time from the United States Navy, **(15)** ..... surveillance system picked up the songs of a lot of different whales. American zoologists subsequently identified the blue whale song among **(16)** ..... .

Now marine biologist, Carol Booker, **(17)** ..... actually seen a blue whale there herself. She has no doubt about what she saw, because they have distinctive fins which are very small for **(18)** ..... size. She says, 'Worldwide they were almost extinct and **(19)** ..... seemed they had completely vanished from the North Atlantic, so you can imagine how I felt actually seeing one! However, it is certainly **(20)** ..... soon to say if it is an indication of a population recovery.' She goes **(21)** ..... to say, 'What it does show **(22)** ..... the importance of this area of the ocean for whales, and **(23)** ..... essential it is to control pollution of the seas.'

Bigger than **(24)** ..... dinosaur known to man, blue whales are the largest animals ever to **(25)** ..... lived on earth. A blue whale is more than six metres long at birth and, **(26)** ..... fully grown, its heart is the **(27)** ..... height as a tall man and weighs as much as a horse.

Part 3

For questions **28–37**, read the text below. Use the word given in capitals at the end of some of the lines to form a word that fits in the gap **in the same line**. There is an example at the beginning (**0**).

Write your answers **IN CAPITAL LETTERS on the separate answer sheet**.

Example:

0	C	H	I	L	D	H	O	O	D								

Marie Curie 1867–1934

Marie Sklodowska was born on 7th November 1867. From early **(0)** ..... ,   **CHILD**

she was fascinated by science and showed great **(28)** ..... for it, as well as   **ENTHUSE**

(29) ..... talent. However, it was her marriage to Pierre Curie in 1895 that   **ORDINARY**

marked the start of a partnership that was to achieve results of world

(30) ....., in particular the discovery of the radioactive metals polonium and   **SIGNIFY**

radium in 1898. By this time Marie Curie, though quiet and unassuming,

was held in great esteem by scientists throughout the world. In 1903 she

became the first woman to receive the Nobel Prize for Physics. Although

the premature death of her husband in 1906 was a bitter blow to her, it

also marked a **(31)** ..... turning point in her career. From this time on, she   **DRAMA**

was to put all her energy into completing alone the work they had

originally **(32)** ..... together.   **TAKE**

Marie Curie won an unprecedented second Nobel Prize for Chemistry

in 1911, for the isolation of pure radium, and for the rest of her

working life she **(33)** ..... promoted the use of radium in treating   **ACT**

illnesses. Her contribution to medical science was **(34)** ....., laying   **STAND**

the **(35)** ..... for research by the scientists who would follow in her   **FOUND**

(36) ..... . Marie Curie's life offers us a profound and fascinating   **FOOT**

(37) ..... into the changing world of women in science and academia.   **SIGHT**

Part 4

For questions **38–42**, think of **one** word only which can be used appropriately in all three sentences. Here is an example (**0**).

Example:

0 The committee decided to .... the money equally between the two charities.

I can't believe that John and Maggie have decided to .... up after 20 years of marriage.

To serve a watermelon you need to .... it down the centre with a sharp knife.

Example:

0	S	P	L	I	T											

Write **only** the missing word **IN CAPITAL LETTERS on the separate answer sheet**.

---

38 We'll have to .... whether or not to let you go to the party; it all depends on how you behave between now and then!

I'm going to .... Lucia later so I'll pass on a message if you want.

I can .... your point but I'm afraid I can't agree with you.

39 If Lisa can't behave .... during the swimming lesson she'll have to leave the pool.

I've never actually met Ramon myself but everyone speaks very .... of him.

The new history teacher's really good; he seems to know his subject ....

40 John's inexperience might .... against him if he applies for the manager's job.

I can always .... on Henry to help out in an emergency.

Mary should .... herself lucky not to have been sacked for arriving late so often.

41 The football team were in .... spirits before the match and felt sure they would win.

Mr Prasad has held a .... position in local government for fifteen years.

Today's cycle race may be cancelled because of the .... winds.

42 The committee .... to discuss the plans for widening the road.

The writer .... the deadline but with only a couple of hours to spare.

The engineers .... so many problems that they had to abandon the project.

Part 5

For questions **43–50**, complete the second sentence so that it has a similar meaning to the first sentence, using the word given. **Do not change the word given**. You must use between **three** and **six** words, including the word given. Here is an example (**0**).

Example:

0 Fernanda refused to wear her sister's old dress.

NOT

Fernanda said that .... her sister's old dress.

The gap can be filled with the words 'she would not wear', so you write:

Example: | **0** | SHE WOULD NOT WEAR

Write the missing words **IN CAPITAL LETTERS on the separate answer sheet**.

---

43 The company is almost certain to get the contract.

EVERY

The company stands .... the contract.

44 Julia says that her sister is the only person to know of our plans to get married.

APART

Julia says that .... knows of our plans to get married.

45 Sven would have called yesterday if he had had more time.

SHORT

Sven didn't call yesterday .... time.

46 Many people believe that Edilson has the ability to become world judo champion.

CAPABLE

Many people believe that Edilson .... the world championship in judo.

47 Hilary was asked to give an explanation for making the mistake.

WHY

Hilary was asked to .... the mistake.

48 In his speech, the Principal did not mention the new language courses.

REFERENCE

In his speech, the Principal .... the new language courses.

49 Lucy was very pleased to be given an award.

DELIGHT

Much to .... given the award.

50 Sam never thought of asking me for my advice.

OCCURRED

It .... me for my advice.

PAPER 4   LISTENING (approximately 40 minutes)

Part 1

You will hear three different extracts. For questions **1–6**, choose the answer (**A**, **B** or **C**) which fits best according to what you hear. There are two questions for each extract.

Extract One

You overhear two friends discussing the work of a well-known sculptor.

1   What does the woman think about his work?

    A   It presents interesting contrasts.

    B   It is under-represented in public places.

    C   It provokes an emotional response in the viewer.

2   When discussing the sculpture wrapped in plastic, the two friends agree that

    A   the wishes of the original artist ought to be respected.

    B   changes to a work of art can inspire fresh thinking.

    C   conservation of works of art should be a priority.

Extract Two

You overhear two friends, Jamie and Miriam, discussing Miriam's future trip to the Gambia, in West Africa.

3   When discussing the trip, Jamie is

    A   reinforcing Miriam's preconceptions of the country.

    B   reminding Miriam of her previous travel experiences.

    C   encouraging Miriam to consider a wider range of activities.

4   Jamie and Miriam agree that tourists

    A   should contribute to the local economy.

    B   should not damage the local environment.

    C   should be sensitive to the traditions of local inhabitants.

Extract Three

You hear part of an interview with a successful financial manager, Frank Ewert, who has just
resigned from his company.

5   What does Frank identify as the main reason for his success?

   A   his ambition to outdo his rivals

   B   his readiness to invest in unfamiliar areas

   C   his determination to increase company profits

6   How does he feel about his clients?

   A   grateful to them for supporting him over the years

   B   keen to encourage them to stay with the company

   C   anxious that they may resent his decision to leave

Part 2

You will hear a tour guide talking to a group of visitors outside an historic country house. For questions **7–14**, complete the sentences.

The history of parks

The first parks appeared in the [**7**] century.

In past centuries, people thought the wilder aspects of

[**8**] were unsafe.

Socially, parks are described as becoming an important [**9**]

[**10**] was considered socially significant in parks.

The fashion for parks tended to lead to the decline in importance of

[**11**] at country houses.

The area around a country house consisted mostly of

[**12**] rather than crops.

The only type of agriculture regularly practised in parks was [**13**]

The 19th-century development of urban parks was influenced

by both rural parks and by [**14**] ideas.

Part 3

You will hear an interview with a woman called Carol Jones, who cycled around the world. For questions **15–20**, choose the answer (**A**, **B**, **C** or **D**) which fits best according to what you hear.

15   When Carol saw a solitary cyclist in India, she felt

    A   inspired to regain proficiency as a cyclist.
    B   surprised at his choice of destination.
    C   determined to join him on his journey.
    D   dissatisfied with what she was doing.

16   Carol says that in the early stages of planning her trip, she worried about

    A   her ability to carry it through.
    B   whether she could afford it.
    C   the practicalities of planning the route.
    D   getting hold of a sufficiently reliable bicycle.

17   How did ordinary people react to Carol when they saw her on the trip?

    A   They were fascinated by what she was doing.
    B   They were unsure whether to offer her hospitality.
    C   They disapproved of her behaviour.
    D   They questioned her true motives.

18   What did Carol find particularly difficult about her journey?

    A   cycling in difficult terrain
    B   dealing with unexpected events
    C   communicating with certain people
    D   coping with disappointments

19   Carol says that one advantage of travelling round the world by bicycle is that

    A   you can stop for a break whenever you like.
    B   you stand out less than other foreign travellers.
    C   you meet other cyclists to exchange ideas with.
    D   you rely less on the goodwill of local people.

20   Looking back on her trip, Carol feels that she should have

    A   learnt more quickly from her mistakes.
    B   had a clearer idea of why she was doing it.
    C   made more effort to raise money for charity.
    D   set herself a less challenging goal.

Part 4

You will hear five short extracts in which people are talking about the experience of winning a competition.

TASK ONE

For questions **21–25**, choose from the list **A–H** each speaker's present occupation.

TASK TWO

For questions **26–30**, choose from the list **A–H** the activity in which each speaker won a competition.

While you listen you must complete both tasks.

A pilot		
B factory worker	Speaker 1	[ ] 21
C lawyer	Speaker 2	[ ] 22
D politician	Speaker 3	[ ] 23
E professional gardener	Speaker 4	[ ] 24
F business manager	Speaker 5	[ ] 25
G artist		
H engineer		

A playing golf		
B nature photography	Speaker 1	[ ] 26
C short-story writing	Speaker 2	[ ] 27
D general knowledge	Speaker 3	[ ] 28
E growing vegetables	Speaker 4	[ ] 29
F playing chess	Speaker 5	[ ] 30
G cookery		
H designing jewellery		

PAPER 5   SPEAKING (15 minutes)

There are two examiners. One (the interlocutor) conducts the test, providing you with the necessary materials and explaining what you have to do. The other examiner (the assessor) is introduced to you, but then takes no further part in the interaction.

Part 1 (3 minutes)

The interlocutor first asks you and your partner a few questions. The interlocutor asks candidates for some information about themselves, then widens the scope of the questions by asking about, e.g. candidates' leisure activities, studies, travel and daily life. Candidates are expected to respond to the interlocutor's questions, and listen to what their partner has to say.

Part 2 (a one-minute 'long turn' for each candidate, plus 30-second response from the second candidate)

You are each given the opportunity to talk for about a minute, and to comment briefly after your partner has spoken.

    The interlocutor gives you a set of pictures and asks you to talk about them for about one minute. It is important to listen carefully to the interlocutor's instructions. The interlocutor then asks your partner a question about your pictures and your partner responds briefly.

    You are then given another set of pictures to look at. Your partner talks about these pictures for about one minute. This time the interlocutor asks you a question about your partner's pictures and you respond briefly.

Part 3 (approximately 4 minutes)

In this part of the test you and your partner are asked to talk together. The interlocutor places a new set of pictures on the table between you. This stimulus provides the basis for a discussion.

    The interlocutor explains what you have to do.

Part 4 (approximately 4 minutes)

The interlocutor asks some further questions, which leads to a more general discussion of what you have talked about in Part 3. You may comment on your partner's answers if you wish.

Test 4

PAPER 1   READING (1 hour 15 minutes)

Part 1

You are going to read three extracts which are all concerned in some way with journalism. For questions **1–6**, choose the answer (**A**, **B**, **C** or **D**) which you think fits best according to the text. Mark your answers **on the separate answer sheet**.

How can I get into music journalism?

If you want to become a music journalist, there are several starting points. One is to have a good knowledge of the greats, because when you write you have to put today's music into context. It isn't enough simply to be familiar with the music of the last five years. Another way is to specialise in a particular type of music, such as folk, country, techno or ambient. And the third starting point is to be a musician. This opens doors to the magazines targeted specifically at musicians rather than a more general readership. There may be opportunities if you don't fit any of those three categories, but it's a competitive marketplace so it's important that in some way you meet the sometimes quite specific needs of the music magazines.

Staff jobs do get advertised from time to time, but your best approach might be to work freelance. This way you can do non-music writing as well, if necessary, to add to your income, and equally importantly, you'll have greater creative freedom by writing for different music magazines. In general they make sure they meet their readers' very specific expectations, and so you may find writing just for one is limiting.

1   What does the writer say about becoming a music journalist?

   A   The most successful journalists find a field that few people specialise in.
   B   Opportunities are mostly limited to certain categories of people.
   C   It is easiest for someone who writes with an individual style.
   D   Traditional opportunities for journalists are now uncommon.

2   In the second paragraph the writer says that each music magazine tends to

   A   publish pieces that fit within a relatively narrow range.
   B   encourage writers to find out what readers expect.
   C   publish pieces that will develop their readers' tastes.
   D   encourage writers to deal with a variety of topics.

Review of *Journalism: A Very Short Introduction* by Ian Hargreaves

This book was published before under a different title and the material has been reissued in the *A Very Short Introduction* … series of titles which aim to give readers a brief, colourful insight into a subject and ignite a passion for further learning and discovery. The series is an alternative to the *Introducing* … series of yesteryear, which briefly introduced readers to people, topics and ideas. *Journalism: A Very Short Introduction* suffers where the *Introducing* … titles excelled. Humour was used by the *Introducing* … series to great effect to draw the reader in and make the subject covered that much more interesting. So much rests on how a subject is taught, and being likened to a textbook, which is a real risk in the present case, would be the kiss of death for a title such as this.

This very short introduction to journalism is bang up to date. Hargreaves wants journalists to question the function they serve and for the public to question journalists. Never has this been more important. Media networks regularly appeal for eyewitness accounts and video from the scenes of breaking news, snippets of the action sent direct to the news studio via mobile phones. We are all becoming journalists. So, where does that leave the journalists? This book does not, in the end, explain what makes a journalist tick. It is rather an instruction manual, and readers are very likely to learn something of interest from it.

3   The writer compares two series of books to suggest that *Journalism: A Very Short Introduction* is not sufficiently

    A   informative for non-specialists.
    B   original in its content.
    C   academic in its style.
    D   entertaining for its readers.

4   According to the second paragraph, the book explores

    A   the role of journalists in modern news coverage.
    B   the motivation of people who become journalists.
    C   the attitudes of ordinary people towards journalism.
    D   the variety of jobs available to journalists.

A closer look at newspaper editorials

Simply put, a newspaper editorial is an article that expresses an opinion. While this single sentence may not seem to do justice to defining what an editorial is, think about this brief definition. What other types of article express this defining characteristic? What other articles actively promote the expression of an opinion? Reviewers may include factual information, so their personal opinions do not totally dominate a review, and news reporters attempt to give 'just the facts' about a situation. Editorials are one of the few types of articles that celebrate the expression of opinion; they are wholly centred on the opinion being presented by the writer and the debate and discussion that the opinion incites.

That said, an editorial writer often attempts to the best of his or her own ability to defend the opinion that is being presented against potential counterarguments – a good editorial does not appear in a vacuum; this defence employs argument, logic, and other appeals to readers in an attempt to achieve a desired effect. The purpose of any given editorial is entirely directed by its writer. Most often, however, editorial writers seek to prove the validity of an opinion through argument, point out something that has been ignored, or simply create discussion about a topic. In sum, most editorials will inevitably involve the defence of an opinion in the hopes of advancing some goal that the writer has in mind.

5   In the first paragraph the writer is

    A   showing how one newspaper differs from another.
    B   recommending a particular category of newspaper writers.
    C   stressing the importance of reading different opinions.
    D   differentiating between various types of newspaper writing.

6   According to the second paragraph, editorial writers are likely to

    A   explain the circumstances in which they could change their opinion.
    B   claim to have opinions that they do not really hold.
    C   take other people's opinions into account.
    D   summarise other writers' opinions on the same topic.

Part 2

You are going to read an extract from a magazine article about Cape Cod. Six paragraphs have been removed from the extract. Choose from the paragraphs **A–G** the one which fits each gap (**7–12**). There is one extra paragraph which you do not need to use. Mark your answers **on the separate answer sheet**.

Where the landscape will do the walking

Despite the growth of tourism in the area, Roger Bray finds there are still undeveloped parts of Cape Cod, an exposed peninsula off the east coast of the USA.

On the fragile outer shore of Cape Cod the pervading sense is of a universe in which nothing stands still. The ocean wages its war of attrition against the shifting sand, which rises from the beach into a steep cliff. Gulls wheel on the wind, swallows dart low over the water's edge.

| 7 | |

The simple reason is that, here, more than in most places, to get off the roads and away from the most easily accessible beaches is to experience the Cape not just as a holiday retreat for urban Americans but as it has always been.

| 8 | |

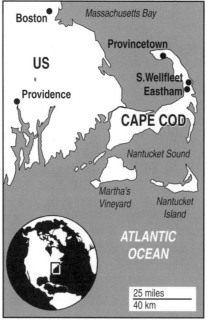

This is mainly because a large swathe of it was established in 1961 as a national park. Our search for recommended hikes took us to the internet – but the maps were hard to follow. We tried bookshops but to no avail. There were books listing walks, to be sure, but the routes they covered were much too short.

| 9 | |

Following its directions made for superb hiking. To cover the whole of the route we wanted to do would have involved linear sections totalling about 50 kilometres. There were circular itineraries, however, varying in length between about 12 and 20 kilometres, though slow going on soft sand makes them seem longer.

| 10 | |

One route took us along the Old King's Highway, once a stagecoach route, into the middle of an eerie swamp of Atlantic white cedar, where the sunlight streamed between shaggy barked trunks and where the park management has built a boardwalk and provided nature information.

| 11 | |

The circuit concluded with an intoxicating hike along the beach. To our right rose the huge sandy cliff, threatening to slide and bury the unwary. Henry Beston, in *The Outermost House*, his lyrical account of a year spent here in the 1920s, describes how, after the cliff was pushed back six metres or so by a momentous storm, the long buried wreckage of ships emerged from it, as fruit from a sliced pudding.

| 12 | |

The shingled Whalewalk Inn was also a delight. It lies behind a white painted picket fence on a leafy road on the fringe of Eastham. It was built in 1830 by Henry Harding, a whaling captain when that industry was at its peak. Later it was used as a farmhouse and a salt works. Nowadays, people also find it a relaxing place to stay.

A It continued to the South Wellfleet sea cliff where Marconi broadcast the first transatlantic wireless message in 1903. The transmitting station was scrapped in 1920 but a model recalls how it looked, its antennae suspended between tall timber masts.

B If we had sauntered a few kilometres from the car park to stand for a while on that great beach, we might still have felt the whirling of the universe. But without a day of serious hiking to sharpen our appetites, would we have appreciated the food so much?

C On the other side, however, there was nothing but ocean, jade green inshore, ink blue farther out, between us and the coast of north-west Spain. Although this was a week of near flawless weather in May, we were lucky to encounter only a handful of other walkers. In high summer, when the roads are clogged and there are queues for restaurant tables, it is harder to find an empty stretch of beach.

D Because, for all the impact of tourism, which nearly triples the population in summer, there are still lonely parts of this storm-scoured, glacial peninsula which have changed little during the last 150 years.

E We tried several of them. Sometimes we were on woodland trails shaded partly by pitch pine and black oak, sometimes on high windy cliffs overlooking the sea, and sometimes on the foreshore, where we were made diminutive by the huge sky and curving beach of white gold sand.

F Henry David Thoreau wrote that 'even the sedentary man here enjoys a breadth of view which is almost equivalent to motion'. Perhaps that was why it proved so difficult to find a guide for long hikes. People must wonder why they need to expend effort when they can let the landscape do the walking.

G Staff at the inquiry desk of the Cape Cod National Seashore's Salt Pond visitor centre were no help, either. But in the centre's bookshop, we struck gold at last. Adam Gamble's *In the Footsteps of Thoreau*, published locally two years ago, has a section tracing the writer's progress in 1849 from Eastham to Race Point Beach, where he turned towards Provincetown, the Cape's outermost community, now a gathering place for whale watchers.

Part 3

You are going to read a magazine article about an artist. For questions **13–19**, choose the answer (**A, B, C** or **D**) which you think fits best according to the text. Mark your answers **on the separate answer sheet**.

Under Sarah's Spell

Sarah Janson is a trompe-l'oeil *artist whose paintings are designed to deceive the eye by creating the illusion of reality. Here she is interviewed by Joanna Watt.*

There cannot be many artists who do not sign their work unless they are asked to. Sarah Janson, a trompe-l'oeil artist, is one. She is not remotely interested in the concept of the artist as creator, let alone that of the artist as genius: 'It's not the artist who is important, but the work,' she states. Janson is so self-deprecating that she would almost like you to believe that her *trompe-l'oeil* works paint themselves.

All of which does not bode well for a magazine interview. 'I just don't like to shout about myself,' she says, and then covers her face in horror when asked if she minds being photographed for the feature. Cut to her sitting room 30 minutes later (a wonderful space in a block of artists' studios in London, filled with paintings and drawings) and you find two women bent double with hysteria. Her confidence gained, the interview becomes a fascinating, amusing (and sometimes hilarious) encounter.

Janson has been a *trompe-l'oeil* artist for sixteen years, after two years' solid drawing at art school ('the best training any artist can ever have'), a degree in graphic illustration and a stint at a publishing house. But illustration never really satisfied her, and she joined a specialist decorator, Jim Smart ('one of the best in his day'). Smart asked her to do one *trompe-l'oeil*, and that was it. 'Suddenly my interest got channelled,' she says. She left to set up on her own, 'not really knowing where I was going, but feeling that I was on the road to somewhere.' Her instinct was right.

Janson's observational skills and fascination with detail (gained through illustrating) proved essential qualities for a *trompe-l'oeil* artist. 'People often ask me where they can learn *trompe-l'oeil*. But no one can teach you. *Trompe-l'oeil* is the school of life. It's all about observation.' She insists (in that self-deprecating way) that she is still learning. 'The moment you think that you've mastered a field you might as well give up.' She is also brutally honest about her 'failings' ('I can't paint bread; it always looks like grey concrete') and is frank about her mathematical abilities. Faced with a huge commission for the domed chapel ceiling at Lulworth Castle, she became totally confused when calculating measurements. 'I thought to myself, "You're not Michelangelo. Who do you think you are?"' This habit

of self-questioning and a reluctance to openly acknowledge her skill has spawned an oddly distanced attitude to her talent. Janson often speaks in the third person: 'When I finished that ceiling, I thought, "Well I didn't do it, she did".'

Of course, her *trompe-l'oeil* schemes can speak for themselves. Janson's work is in a league of its own, far above those who have jumped on the bandwagon (the art of *trompe-l'oeil* has experienced something of a revival, but not with entirely satisfactory results) and she has a string of major corporate and private commissions behind her. Much of her work is inspired by architecture or made for architectural settings. There is the *trompe-l'oeil* dining room for one client, based on the façade of a Venetian palazzo, and the painting at the end of a corridor in a flat, which gives the illusion that you can step into two further rooms.

There is always a danger with *trompe-l'oeil*, though, that once you get the joke, your attention is lost, something of which Janson is acutely aware. '*Trompe-l'oeil* has to do two things. First, it must draw you in; it's got to trick you. Secondly, it has to hold you and then engage your imagination. That is the most important part.'

While *trompe-l'oeil* has to be clever, it must also, Janson believes, be personal to the client. 'I love the interaction with clients; that is where the ideas are born,' she says. 'Without the rapport, the job of creating a *trompe-l'oeil* scheme becomes rather difficult. Some clients have firm ideas about what they want; others do not. You have to be willing to listen. You have to get inside a client's imagination.' Many have become friends, not least because Janson practically lives with them if she works on site.

Janson is generous in praise of her clients. 'I am very grateful for the mad ones who have let me loose on their walls,' she confesses. And, they too, seem delighted with her, which is why she is constantly busy – despite her inclination to play down her talent. 'I really don't like to shout about myself,' she repeats at the end. 'Like my work, I am very restrained. I don't want it to shout. You become bored with things that shout.' True, perhaps, but you could never really become bored with Janson or her work. It certainly deserves to become better known, and I am prepared to incur her wrath while I blow her trumpet.

13 After spending time with Janson, the interviewer concludes that

    A Janson has little faith in journalists.
    B Janson dislikes interviews in her home.
    C her initial doubts about Janson were wrong.
    D her first questions to Janson were threatening.

14 What motivated Janson to start her own business as a *trompe-l'oeil* artist?

    A It was something she was well qualified to do.
    B She was unhappy with her previous employer.
    C She was convinced it was what she wanted to do.
    D It was something that would help her achieve her ambitions.

15 What advice does Janson give to people interested in becoming *trompe-l'oeil* artists?

    A It would be a mistake to become over-confident.
    B Practice is the only way to improve shortcomings.
    C Experience in different art forms helps develop essential skills.
    D A lot can be gained from looking at the work of other artists.

16 What point does the interviewer make about Janson's work in the fifth paragraph?

    A It is of an exceptional quality.
    B Some people regard it as strange.
    C It is better suited to small locations.
    D Janson regrets some of the commissions she has taken on.

17 What does Janson say about *trompe-l'oeil* as an art form?

    A It has limited commercial appeal.
    B The most successful pieces avoid humour.
    C A small number of people accept it as genuine art.
    D The difficulty lies in sustaining people's interest.

18 What does Janson say about her clients?

    A She prefers to work with clients who have a lot of imagination.
    B Some clients have ideas which are less practical than others.
    C She is reluctant to take on commissions if she cannot agree with the client.
    D A commission is easier if you can discover what kind of ideas the client has.

19 What does the interviewer say in the final paragraph?

    A She is puzzled by the way Janson describes her clients.
    B She realises that Janson may not like what she has written about her.
    C She is sure that certain types of art soon lose their appeal.
    D She feels that trompe-l'oeil is unlikely to become a more popular art form.

Part 4

You are going to read an article from a book about being a shopkeeper. For questions **20–34**, choose from the sections (**A–E**). The sections may be chosen more than once.

Mark your answers **on the separate answer sheet**.

Note: When more than one answer is required, these may be given **in any order**.

In which section(s) of the text are the following mentioned?

indications of a lack of genuine enthusiasm for shopkeeping	**20**
reactions that make difficult situations even worse	**21**
a negative outcome that is not the fault of the shopkeeper	**22**
an assumption about the financial rewards of shopkeeping	**23** **24**
a belief that shopkeepers should always make sure they appear at ease	**25**
a situation that makes shopkeeping even more risky than usual	**26**
shopkeepers failing to put the correct value on what they deal in	**27**
an uncomfortable fact that cannot be disputed	**28**
shopkeepers who are particularly good at only one aspect of their work	**29**
shopkeepers who deal in goods for which there is not much demand	**30**
a disadvantage of shopkeeping that shopkeepers of all kinds experience	**31**
actions taken by shopkeepers without sufficient consideration	**32**
something that others assume shopkeepers will do for them	**33**
matters that shopkeepers must constantly be dealing with	**34**

HOW TO RUN A SHOP

Ian Maitland offers a practical survival guide to retailing today.

A   Shopkeeping, whether in a bakery or toystore, differs greatly from how people on the other side of the counter fondly imagine it to be. In theory, there are many positive aspects: you are your own boss and are able to choose which hours, days and weeks to work; it is an almost idyllic existence with little to do except sit behind a counter each day reading a book with one hand whilst raking in money with the other; all you need to do is smile sweetly at customers as you take their money and you'll be sitting on a goldmine. In reality, there are innumerable negative aspects which people do not always recognise. Whatever the trade, the hours are long – far lengthier than most employees ever have to work. Shopkeeping is physically demanding as well, in most trades. Even worse, shopkeeping is mentally stressful. You have to be forever vigilant to keep costs down and profits up, buying and selling at the right prices, paying invoices and chasing payments at the correct times. Through all of this you need to keep smiling, staying cheerful for your customers. Don't forget you're at the sharp end too: suppliers, employees and customers with problems will come to you, expecting their difficulties to be solved immediately.

B   Shopkeeping is above all financially hazardous, especially in recessionary times. Although statistics vary, it is undeniable that most small, independent shops close down within a few years of opening their doors. Some retailers find themselves unsuited to the lifestyle, or perhaps they make too many errors, such as insufficient funding, a poorly chosen business, too much slow-selling stock, inadequate control systems and so on. Others do everything properly but find circumstances are against them; perhaps a nationally known store opens nearby, or a recession takes hold of the market. Do not be under any illusions: even if your approach is perfect, the unforgiving statistics suggest you are as likely to fail as to succeed – and soon!

C   If you are determined to press ahead with becoming a shopkeeper, first consider all the qualities required to be a success and whether or not you possess them in abundance. You need a mix of self-confidence and willpower to get a business off the ground and keep it going year after year. Your temperament is important: losing your temper with stonewalling bank managers, slow-to-deliver suppliers and confused customers will be counterproductive. Suddenly deciding to carry a new range of goods, hold a sale or drop an existing service without fully appraising the likely pros and cons of different courses of action is a recipe for impending setbacks or out-and-out disaster.

D   Some knowledge and experience of your proposed trade, and retailing in general, are essential if you plan to start a business from scratch and very desirable if you are going to purchase an existing concern. The complete novice who has never worked in the chosen trade nor stood behind a counter in his or her life has almost no chance of success. There is much to learn in so little time, and the pitfalls are many and varied. The winning retailer has to be a good all-rounder, able enough to spot a suitable site and quality premises, charm a bank manager, suppliers and customers, keep accurate books and records, advertise his or her business and so on. Too often, retailers have a single predominant skill to the exclusion of others. They may have first-class products but do not possess the social skills required to sell them, or buy popular goods from wholesalers but under- or overprice or mistreat them. You ought to be a jack of all trades – and a master of them all too.

E   Think about your motives for going into the retail trade, to make sure that they are truly appropriate. Ideally, you should almost burn inside to be your own boss, knowing you have what it takes – temperament, skills and so forth – to make a go of your down-to-earth ideas. It should be a lifelong ambition. A brooding sense of feeling unfulfilled in a job, the fear or reality of unemployment, a surplus of redundancy money to spend, a desire to do 'something': all these are inappropriate reasons which smack of uncertainty and half-heartedness. These are not factors that should be driving you into shopkeeping. Then consider your goals, being certain that they are wholly realistic. Earning a reasonable living, equal to or slightly above the average industrial wage, for a hard day's graft is achievable. 'Having a great time', 'taking things easy', 'having a bit of a laugh' and 'making a fortune' – all of which are real quotes from would-be retailers – reveal attitudes that are likely to lead to abject failure, and deservedly so.

PAPER 2   WRITING (1 hour 30 minutes)

Part 1

You **must** answer this question. Write your answer in **180–220** words in an appropriate style.

---

1 While you were on holiday in England, you visited the museum at Hintonbury and have been asked for your opinion about it.

Read the advertisement for the museum, on which you have made some notes, and a note you were given with your ticket. Then, **using the information appropriately**, write a letter to the museum director saying what you enjoyed about the visit, explaining what was disappointing and suggesting ways to attract more visitors to the museum.

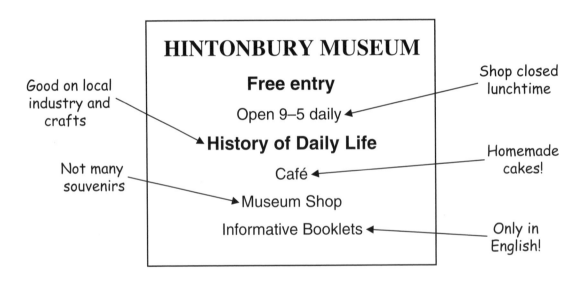

Write your **letter**. You should use your own words as far as possible. You do not need to include postal addresses.

Part 2

Choose **one** of the following writing tasks. Your answer should follow exactly the instructions given. Write approximately **220–260** words.

---

2   A technology magazine, *International Technology Today*, has asked its readers to submit articles on the impact of mobile phones on modern society. In your article, you should discuss the different personal and business uses of mobile phones and assess the advantages and disadvantages of this technology.

Write your **article**.

3   Your town is hoping to host a sports event next year, which will attract competitors from other countries. The organisers of this sports event need to ensure that the chosen venue has an adequate range of facilities for visitors. Write a proposal to the organising committee to persuade them that your town is a suitable venue. Your proposal should include information on accommodation, transport and entertainment.

Write your **proposal**.

4   You have been asked to write an information sheet giving advice to students from abroad about how to get the most out of studying in your college. The title is *Studying and Student Life* and the information sheet must include advice relating to:
  •   methods of study
  •   suitable types of accommodation
  •   social life.

Write your **information sheet**.

5   Answer **one** of the following two questions based on **one** of the titles below.

(a) Adriana Trigiani: *Big Stone Gap*

You have been asked to write an article on *Big Stone Gap* for a web site. Your article should focus on the two scenes of the story which made the strongest impression on you. Comment on how the people involved in these scenes must have been feeling and explain why the scenes made such a strong impression on you.

Write your **article**.

(b) Dick Francis: *In the Frame*

Your English teacher is trying to decide on a book or film to study with a language class and has asked you to write a report on *In the Frame*. Your report should briefly describe *In the Frame* and should comment on whether it would be a useful and an enjoyable choice for studying in an English class.

Write your **report**.

PAPER 3   USE OF ENGLISH (1 hour)

Part 1

For questions **1–12**, read the article below and decide which answer (**A, B, C** or **D**) best fits each gap. There is an example at the beginning (**0**).

Mark your answers **on the separate answer sheet**.

Example:

0 A tries   **B** tests   **C** attempts   **D** aims

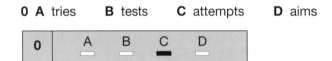

We really can tell if we are being watched

Stories about how people somehow know when they are being watched have been going around for years. However, few **(0)** ..... have been made to investigate the phenomenon scientifically. Now, with the completion of the largest ever study of the so-called *staring effect*, there is impressive evidence that this is a recognisable and **(1)** ..... sixth sense. The study **(2)** ..... hundreds of children. For the experiments, they sat with their eyes covered and with their backs to other children, who were told to either stare at them or look away. The results consistently showed that the children who could not see were able to **(3)** ..... when they were being stared at. In a total of 18,000 trials **(4)** ..... worldwide, the children **(5)** ..... sensed when they were being watched almost 70% of the time. The experiment was repeated with the **(6)** ..... precaution of putting the children who were being watched outside the room, **(7)** ..... from the starers by the windows. This was done just in case there was some **(8)** ..... going on, with the children telling each other whether they were looking or not. This **(9)** ..... the possibility of sounds being **(10)** ..... between the children. The results, though less impressive, were more or less the same. Dr Sheldrake, the biologist who designed the study, believes that the results are **(11)** ..... enough to find out through further experiments **(12)** ..... how the staring effect might actually come about.

---

1 **A** genuine   **B** accepted   **C** received   **D** sure

2 **A** involved   **B** contained   **C** comprised   **D** enclosed

3 **A** find   **B** notice   **C** tell   **D** reveal

4 **A** worked over   **B** worked through **C** carried on   **D** carried out

5 **A** correctly   **B** exactly   **C** thoroughly   **D** perfectly

6 **A** attached   **B** added   **C** connected   **D** increased

7 **A** separated   **B** parted   **C** split   **D** divided

8 **A** pretending   **B** lying   **C** cheating   **D** deceiving

9 **A** prevented   **B** omitted   **C** evaded   **D** ended

10 **A** delivered   **B** transported   **C** transmitted   **D** distributed

11 **A** satisfying   **B** convincing   **C** concluding   **D** persuading

12 **A** really   **B** carefully   **C** definitely   **D** precisely

Part 2

For questions **13–27**, read the article below and think of the word which best fits each gap. Use only **one** word in each gap. There is an example at the beginning (**0**).

Write your answers **IN CAPITAL LETTERS on the separate answer sheet.**

Example: | **0** | S | I | N | C | E | | | | | | | | | | | |

The toughest runners

There are a few runners who have completed every London Marathon **(0)** ..... the first race in 1981. They are the toughest runners of **(13)** ..... . These athletes, **(14)** ..... honour of both their mental and physical strength, have been given a permanent entry in the event for the rest of their lives, provided that they do not miss a year. Other people have run the race faster or under greater handicaps, **(15)** ..... these are athletes with a mission. For **(16)** ..... , the annual event is a way of life, not just a worthy fund-raising exercise **(17)** ..... a single challenge. Bill O'Connor is one of these runners. In **(18)** ..... case, running is a daily ritual which began in New Zealand **(19)** ..... , as a youngster, he pounded along the wet sand on the edge of the Tasman Sea. Now aged fifty, **(20)** ..... working as a mathematics teacher at a school in London, he retains his fascination **(21)** ..... the London Marathon and the activity of running. He says, 'When the first London Marathon was held, I thought **(22)** ..... myself that here was a challenge. I thought that if there was only going to be one race, I wanted to have run in **(23)** ..... .' But the London Marathon went **(24)** ..... to become the most impressive success story in British sport and Bill O'Connor has been a constant part of it. **(25)** ..... he ever felt that he would fail to finish? 'In 1985. It was a beautiful day and I started running much **(26)** ..... fast for the first mile and got worried. So I slowed down for the next mile. Yet **(27)** ..... I expected I would take at least four hours, I finished in two hours thirty-four minutes and twenty-nine seconds.' It is his best time so far.

Part 3

For questions **28–37**, read the text below. Use the word given in capitals at the end of some of the lines to form a word that fits in the gap **in the same line**. There is an example at the beginning (**0**).

Write your answers **IN CAPITAL LETTERS on the separate answer sheet**.

Example:

0	D	E	L	I	G	H	T	F	U	L								

Gulangyu

One of the most **(0)** ..... places in China is a small island called Gulangyu.   **DELIGHT**

It is often called 'piano island' because of the large number of **(28)** .....   **MUSIC**

who live there. But perhaps Gulangyu's greatest appeal is that although

it has 20,000 permanent **(29)** ....., mostly living in a central community   **RESIDE**

one kilometre wide, there are no high-rise buildings and motor vehicles

and bicycles are banned. Personal **(30)** ..... are carried, or pushed on   **BELONG**

small wagons.

While Gulangyu is a popular day trip for people from the neighbouring

island of Xiamen, it seems a relatively **(31)** ..... destination for visitors   **DISCOVER**

from elsewhere in China or further afield. One reason why Gulangyu has

not been beseiged by Chinese visitors is its **(32)** ..... location. Several   **GEOGRAPHY**

mountain ranges on mainland China mean that road and rail **(33)** .....   **CONNECT**

from the prosperous cities to its east and south are very slow. Air travel,

via Xiamen airport, is a possibility, but it is too expensive for the majority

of visitors.

There are certainly enough attractions for those tourists who do arrive,

including parks, an aquarium and souvenir shops. There are also some

excellent restaurants, though they may charge **(34)** ..... more than those   **CONSIDER**

found in other, less **(35)** ..... parts of the country. However, one key   **PICTURE**

tourist business that is not much in **(36)** ..... is hotels – there are only a   **EVIDENT**

(37) ..... in the centre of the island.   **HAND**

Part 4

For questions **38–42**, think of **one** word only which can be used appropriately in all three sentences. Here is an example (**0**).

Example:

0 The committee decided to .... the money equally between the two charities.

I can't believe that John and Maggie have decided to .... up after 20 years of marriage.

To serve a watermelon you need to .... it down the centre with a sharp knife.

Example: | **0** | | S | P | L | I | T | | | | | | | | | | | | | |

Write **only** the missing word **IN CAPITAL LETTERS on the separate answer sheet**.

---

38 Once the management has decided on the .... of events for the training day, a letter will be sent to all staff.

The President gave the .... for a holiday to be declared to celebrate the birth of his son.

I'd asked them to deliver the fridge but it never arrived, and when I enquired the company said they had no trace of my ....

39 After months of intensive training, Glyn thought he was in with a .... chance of winning a medal at the games.

The manager made a .... argument for lowering the price of the company's product.

The .... currents in the bay make sailing tricky even in perfect weather conditions.

40 They had a long wait at the airport so they .... the time doing puzzles.

Jan .... the contract to me so that I could check its accuracy.

The car that .... us on the motorway was going far too fast.

41 You need to .... on the right side of Mrs Smith – she can be very difficult if she gets annoyed with you.

The doctor says I'll need to .... on taking the tablets for at least a week.

You can .... that bicycle for as long as you want – I never use it these days.

42 The film examines the theme of what it is like to live in a strange .... far from home.

He owned a large amount of .... in the north of the country, and was said to be extremely rich.

The .... in that area is very fertile, and supports a wide variety of crops.

Part 5

For questions **43–50**, complete the second sentence so that it has a similar meaning to the first sentence, using the word given. **Do not change the word given.** You must use between **three** and **six** words, including the word given. Here is an example (**0**).

Example:

0 Fernanda refused to wear her sister's old dress.

NOT

Fernanda said that .... her sister's old dress.

The gap can be filled with the words 'she would not wear', so you write:

Example:	0	SHE WOULD NOT WEAR

Write the missing words **IN CAPITAL LETTERS on the separate answer sheet**.

---

43 Pat does not intend to have a holiday this year.

INTENTION

Pat has .... on holiday this year.

44 John thought it was very strange that Fred had not answered his letter.

FAILURE

John thought that .... his letter was very strange.

45 I think it was a mistake to lend your car to Joe.

SHOULD

I don't think .... your car to Joe.

46 By the end of the month, it will be two years since Hendrik came to England.

FOR

By the end of the month, Hendrik .... two years.

47 Despite all their efforts, they could not get the old car to start.

HARD

No matter ...., they couldn't get the old car to start.

48 'I'm sorry, but there's no way I'm going to sleep on the floor,' said Naomi.

CLEAR

Naomi made .... prepared to sleep on the floor.

49 I don't think you'll have much difficulty understanding the local dialect.

FIND

I don't think .... to understand the local dialect.

50 Mats promised to ring as soon as he got home.

MOMENT

Mats said that .... he got home.

PAPER 4   LISTENING (approximately 40 minutes)

Part 1

You will hear three different extracts. For questions **1–6**, choose the answer (**A**, **B** or **C**) which fits best according to what you hear. There are two questions for each extract.

Extract One

You hear part of a radio programme about making a cake called a Swiss Roll.

1   What did the man have to do before he could make the cake?

    A   make space in his kitchen

    B   choose the most suitable recipe

    C   buy the correct type of baking tray

2   How did he feel while he was making the cake?

    A   confident that it would turn out well

    B   pleased to be trying something new

    C   surprised at how easy the process seemed to be

Extract Two

You hear part of an interview with the novelist Joanna Marley, who is talking about the notebooks she uses.

3   What does Joanna say about the notebook she's chosen for her next novel?

    A   It's taken a long time to find one she's happy with.

    B   Its outward appearance matches the novel's theme.

    C   It's finally inspired her to start doing some research.

4   How does Joanna feel about her notebook once she is actually writing her novel?

    A   reluctant to follow her tutor's advice

    B   worried if she doesn't have it with her

    C   unwilling to make much reference to it

Extract Three

You hear a man and a woman discussing professional tennis players.

5   Which aspect of professional tennis would the woman find most stressful?

   A   the unpredictability of the weather

   B   the hostile comments from people in the crowd

   C   the loneliness of being on court for a long time

6   The man is particularly impressed by professional tennis players'

   A   use of relaxation techniques.

   B   mental preparation prior to the match.

   C   ability to stay calm at critical moments.

Part 2

You will hear a journalist called Peter Smith talking about a trip he made to the Arctic seas around the North Pole. For questions **7–14**, complete the sentences.

Arctic trip

After reading a book called

	7

, Peter decided to sail to the North Pole.

Peter says that when sailing in this part of the world, you feel as if you are

	8

Peter says it is essential to have the necessary

	9

on board to deal with problems.

In summer, the temperature of the water always remains

	10

at the surface.

It is necessary to have

	11

in the cabin.

The crew couldn't explain why there were

	12

in the sea.

Peter was disappointed not to see any

	13

during the trip.

People usually visit the area as part of

	14

and see very few places.

Part 3

You will hear part of an interview with Norman Cowley, a well-known novelist and biographer. For questions **15–20**, choose the answer (**A, B, C** or **D**) which fits best according to what you hear.

15 How does Norman Cowley feel about his first novel?

    A   proud of the directness of the writing
    B   pleased by the way the characters interacted
    C   worried by the over-refined style he used then
    D   sad that he could never write anything like it again

16 What was Norman Cowley's reaction to one very bad review of his second novel?

    A   He was surprised as he thought this book was well written.
    B   He thought the detailed criticisms of the book were unjustified.
    C   He thought the review was written in a clever and amusing style.
    D   He did not regard the critic as well qualified to judge his work.

17 What value does Norman Cowley see in book reviews now?

    A   They encourage writers to try new subjects.
    B   They motivate less committed writers.
    C   They give young writers long-term guidance.
    D   They are part of a necessary selection process.

18 Norman Cowley thinks that if a writer uses people he knows well in a book,

    A   those characters will be very realistic.
    B   it will become rather tedious to write.
    C   readers will find the dialogue very natural.
    D   the writer will have to alter them in some way.

19 Norman Cowley believes that some modern novels

    A   are much too violent.
    B   contain too much fantasy.
    C   don't analyse the characters sufficiently.
    D   don't describe the setting adequately.

20 What does Norman Cowley see as the main thing a novel should give the reader?

    A   psychological theories
    B   a new angle on life
    C   a thrilling story
    D   beautiful language

Part 4

You will hear five short extracts in which people are talking about the means of escape they use to cope with the demands of their working lives.

TASK ONE

For questions **21–25**, choose from the list **A–H** what each speaker finds demanding about their work.

TASK TWO

For questions **26–30**, choose from the list **A–H** what attracts the speakers to their different means of escape.

While you listen you must complete both tasks.

TASK ONE		TASK TWO	
A emotional involvement		**A** the feeling of being artistic	
B an excess of information		**B** the warmth of the relationships	
C clashes of personality		**C** the fulfilment of a childhood ambition	
D everyday problems		**D** the idea of taking a risk	
E arguments about procedures		**E** the chance to overindulge yourself	
F extended working hours		**F** the change of activities	
G being in the public eye		**G** the luxury provided	
H lack of physical space		**H** the spirit of co-operation	

Speaker 1	21	Speaker 1	26
Speaker 2	22	Speaker 2	27
Speaker 3	23	Speaker 3	28
Speaker 4	24	Speaker 4	29
Speaker 5	25	Speaker 5	30

PAPER 5   SPEAKING (15 minutes)

There are two examiners. One (the interlocutor) conducts the test, providing you with the necessary materials and explaining what you have to do. The other examiner (the assessor) is introduced to you, but then takes no further part in the interaction.

Part 1 (3 minutes)

The interlocutor first asks you and your partner a few questions. The interlocutor asks candidates for some information about themselves, then widens the scope of the questions by asking about, e.g. candidates' leisure activities, studies, travel and daily life. Candidates are expected to respond to the interlocutor's questions, and listen to what their partner has to say.

Part 2 (a one-minute 'long turn' for each candidate, plus 30-second response from the second candidate)

You are each given the opportunity to talk for about a minute, and to comment briefly after your partner has spoken.

The interlocutor gives you a set of pictures and asks you to talk about them for about one minute. It is important to listen carefully to the interlocutor's instructions. The interlocutor then asks your partner a question about your pictures and your partner responds briefly.

You are then given another set of pictures to look at. Your partner talks about these pictures for about one minute. This time the interlocutor asks you a question about your partner's pictures and you respond briefly.

Part 3 (approximately 4 minutes)

In this part of the test you and your partner are asked to talk together. The interlocutor places a new set of pictures on the table between you. This stimulus provides the basis for a discussion.

The interlocutor explains what you have to do.

Part 4 (approximately 4 minutes)

The interlocutor asks some further questions, which leads to a more general discussion of what you have talked about in Part 3. You may comment on your partner's answers if you wish.

Paper 5 Frames

Test 1

Note: In the examination, there will be both an assessor and an interlocutor in the room. The visual material for **Test 1** appears on pages C1 and C2 (Part 2), and C3 (Part 3).

Part 1 3 minutes (5 minutes for groups of three)

Interlocutor:	Good morning/afternoon/evening. My name is .... and this is my colleague ....

And your names are?

Can I have your mark sheets, please?

Thank you.

First of all, we'd like to know something about you.

Select one or two questions and ask candidates in turn, as appropriate.

- Where are you from?
- What do you do here/there?
- How long have you been studying English?
- What do you enjoy most about learning English?

Select one or more questions from any of the following categories, as appropriate.

Learning

- Do you prefer studying on your own or with other people? ...... (Why?)
- How important have teachers been in your life so far?

Places

- What is the most memorable place you have ever visited?
- Which is the most important room in your house? ...... (Why is that?)

Health and fitness

- What do you do to keep fit?
- If you had the opportunity to learn a new sport, what would it be? ...... (Why?)

Part 2   4 minutes (6 minutes for groups of three)

Making music

Moments of peace and quiet

Interlocutor:	In this part of the test, I'm going to give each of you three pictures. I'd like you to talk about them on your own for about a minute, and also to answer a question briefly about your partner's pictures.
	(Candidate A), it's your turn first. Here are your pictures. They show **people making music.**
	Indicate the pictures on page C1 to the candidates.
	I'd like you to compare two of the pictures, and say how the people might be feeling, and what part music might play in their lives.
	All right?
Candidate A:	[*1 minute*]
Interlocutor:	Thank you.
	(Candidate B), which of these people do you think seems to be enjoying their music the most?
Candidate B:	[*Approximately 30 seconds*]
Interlocutor:	Thank you.
	Now, *(Candidate B)*, here are your pictures. They show **moments of peace and quiet.**
	Indicate the pictures on page C2 to the candidates.
	I'd like you to compare two of the pictures, and say how the people might be feeling, and why moments like these might be necessary in their lives.
	All right?
Candidate B:	[*1 minute*]
Interlocutor:	Thank you.
	(Candidate A), which picture do you think best illustrates the idea of peace and quiet?
Candidate A:	[*Approximately 30 seconds*]
Interlocutor:	Thank you.

Parts 3 and 4   8 minutes (12 minutes for groups of three)

Hopes and dreams

Part 3

Interlocutor:	Now, I'd like you to talk about something together for about three minutes. *(5 minutes for groups of three)*
	Here are some pictures of people who have different hopes and dreams.
	Indicate the pictures on page C3 to the candidates.
	First, talk to each other about how difficult it might be for these people to make their hopes and dreams come true. Then decide which two are most likely to become reality.
	All right?
Candidates:	[*3 minutes (5 minutes for groups of three)*]
Interlocutor:	Thank you.

Part 4

Interlocutor: *Select any of the following questions as appropriate:*

- How important is it for people to have hopes and dreams?
- What hopes for the future of the world would you like to see become reality?
- What aspects of life today would have seemed impossible to people in the past?
- Our hopes and dreams change as we get older. What differences are there between children's and adults' dreams?
- Instead of accepting the world as it is, what could we do to make it a better place?

Thank you. That is the end of the test.

> *Select any of the following prompts as appropriate:*
> - What do you think?
> - Do you agree?
> - How about you?

Test 2

Note: In the examination, there will be both an assessor and an interlocutor in the room. The visual material for **Test 2** appears on pages C4, C5 (Part 2), and C6 (Part 3).

Part 1   3 minutes (5 minutes for groups of three)

Interlocutor: Good morning/afternoon/evening. My name is .... and this is my colleague ....

And your names are?

Can I have your mark sheets, please?

Thank you.

First of all, we'd like to know something about you.

Select one or two questions and ask candidates in turn, as appropriate.

- Where are you from?
- What do you do here/there?
- How long have you been studying English?
- What do you enjoy most about learning English?

Select one or more questions from any of the following categories, as appropriate.

Daily life

- How important is the computer in your daily life?
- Is it easy for you to find time to relax every day? ......
  (Why?/Why not?)

Friends

- Do you and your friends share the same interests? ...... (Is this a good thing?)
- Do you think you will still have the same friends in ten years' time?

The future

- What do you think you will be doing in five years' time?
- Are you excited or worried about the future? ...... (Why?)

Part 2   4 minutes (6 minutes for groups of three)

Aiming for perfection

Saying goodbye

Interlocutor:	In this part of the test, I'm going to give each of you three pictures. I'd like you to talk about them on your own for about a minute, and also to answer a question briefly about your partner's pictures.
	(Candidate A), it's your turn first. Here are your pictures. They show **people aiming for perfection.**
	Indicate the pictures on page C4 to the candidates.
	I'd like you to compare two of the pictures, and say how difficult it might have been for these people to acquire their skills, and what might have motivated them to aim for perfection.
	All right?
Candidate A:	[*1 minute*]
Interlocutor:	Thank you.
	(Candidate B), which of these people do you think has put the most effort into acquiring their skills?
Candidate B:	[*Approximately 30 seconds*]
Interlocutor:	Thank you.
	Now, *(Candidate B)*, here are your pictures. They show **people saying goodbye.**
	Indicate the pictures on C5 to the candidates.
	I'd like you to compare two of the pictures, and say why the people might be saying goodbye, and how they might be feeling.
	All right?
Candidate B:	[*1 minute*]
Interlocutor:	Thank you.
	(Candidate A), which of these situations do you think the people will remember most?
Candidate A:	[*Approximately 30 seconds*]
Interlocutor:	Thank you.

Parts 3 and 4   8 minutes (12 minutes for groups of three)

Take more exercise

Part 3

Interlocutor:	Now, I'd like you to talk about something together for about three minutes. *(5 minutes for groups of three)*
	I'd like you to imagine that a leaflet is being produced to encourage people living in the cities to take more exercise. Here are some pictures which are being considered for the leaflet.
	Indicate the pictures on page C6 to the candidates.
	First, talk to each other about how successful these pictures would be in encouraging city people to take more exercise. Then decide which two pictures should be included in the leaflet.
	All right?
Candidates:	[*3 minutes (5 minutes for groups of three)*]
Interlocutor:	Thank you.

Part 4

Interlocutor: *Select any of the following questions as appropriate:*

- What other ways are there of keeping fit and healthy?
- How far do you agree that you have to spend a lot of money to stay fit and healthy?
- Some people say that nowadays we are more interested in looking after ourselves than looking after others. What's your opinion?
- With new technology, people will be able to do almost anything they want to without leaving their homes. What would the disadvantages of this be?
- Modern medicine is making it possible for people to live longer. Do you think this is a good thing? ...... (Why?/Why not?)

Select any of the following prompts as appropriate:

- What do you think?
- Do you agree?
- How about you?

Thank you. That is the end of the test.

Test 3

Note: In the examination, there will be both an assessor and an interlocutor in the room. The visual material for **Test 3** appears on pages C7 and C8 (Part 2), and C9 (Part 3).

Part 1   3 minutes (5 minutes for groups of three)

Interlocutor: Good morning/afternoon/evening. My name is .... and this is my colleague ....

And your names are?

Can I have your mark sheets, please?

Thank you.

First of all, we'd like to know something about you.

Select one or two questions and ask candidates in turn, as appropriate.

- Where are you from?
- What do you do here/there?
- How long have you been studying English?
- What do you enjoy most about learning English?

Select one or more questions from any of the following categories, as appropriate.

Personal experience

- In what ways do you hope to use your English in the future?
- Looking back in your life, what has been a memorable event for you?

The media

- Do you prefer watching films at home or in the cinema? ...... (Why?)
- How important are newspapers for you? ...... (Why do you say that?)

Travel

- What advice would you give to someone coming to visit your country?
- Would you consider going on holiday on your own? ...... (Why?/Why not?)

Part 2   4 minutes (6 minutes for groups of three)

Measuring things

Different environments

Interlocutor:	In this part of the test, I'm going to give each of you three pictures. I'd like you to talk about them on your own for about a minute, and also to answer a question briefly about your partner's pictures.
	(Candidate A), it's your turn first. Here are your pictures. They show **people measuring things**.
	Indicate the pictures on page C7 to the Candidates.
	I'd like you to compare two of the pictures, and say why the people might be measuring these things, and how important it is for them to be accurate.
	All right?
Candidate A:	[*1 minute*]
Interlocutor:	Thank you.
	(Candidate B), in which situation do you think it is most important to be accurate?
Candidate B:	[*Approximately 30 seconds*]
Interlocutor:	Thank you.
	Now, *(Candidate B)*, here are your pictures. They show **people exploring different environments**.
	Indicate the pictures on page C8 to the candidates.
	I'd like you to compare two of the pictures, and say what you think makes people want to explore, and what risks they may be taking.
	All right?
Candidate B:	[*1 minute*]
Interlocutor:	Thank you.
	(Candidate A), which of these people do you think is taking the greatest risk?
Candidate A:	[*Approximately 30 seconds*]
Interlocutor:	Thank you.

Parts 3 and 4   8 minutes (12 minutes for groups of three)

Worldwide issues

Part 3

Interlocutor:	Now, I'd like you to talk about something together for about three minutes. *(5 minutes for groups of three)*
	Here are some pictures showing worldwide issues which worry people nowadays.
	Indicate the pictures on page C9 to the Candidates.
	First, talk to each other about why people find these issues worrying. Then decide in which two cases improvements are most needed.
	All right?
Candidates:	[3 minutes *(5 minutes for groups of three)*]
Interlocutor:	Thank you.

Part 4

Interlocutor: *Select any of the following questions as appropriate:*

- What do you think we as individuals can do to make improvements to our world?
- How important is it for us to understand different cultures and customs?
- It's a fact that today most of the world's wealth is in the hands of relatively few people. What could be done about this?
- Do you think human beings ever learn from the mistakes they have made in the past? ...... (Why?/Why not?)
- One day all the nations of the world might live together peacefully. How likely do you think this is?

Thank you. That is the end of the test.

> *Select any of the following prompts as appropriate:*
>
> - What do you think?
> - Do you agree?
> - How about you?

Test 4

Note: In the examination, there will be both an assessor and an interlocutor in the room. The visual material for **Test 4** appears on pages C10 and C11 (Part 2), and C12 (Part 3).

Part 1   3 minutes (5 minutes for groups of three)

Interlocutor: Good morning/afternoon/evening. My name is .... and this is my colleague ....

And your names are?

Can I have your mark sheets, please?

Thank you.

First of all, we'd like to know something about you.

Select one or two questions and ask candidates in turn, as appropriate.

- Where are you from?
- What do you do here/there?
- How long have you been studying English?
- What do you enjoy most about learning English?

Select one or more questions from any of the following categories, as appropriate.

Leisure

- What do you do to relax after a busy day?
- How important is music in your life?

Travel

- Where would you like to go for your next holiday? ...... (Why?)
- What do you enjoy most about being on holiday?

People

- Who has had the greatest influence on your life so far? ...... (Why?)
- How easy is it for you to meet new people?

Part 2 4 minutes (6 minutes for groups of three)

Happiness

Joint efforts

Interlocutor:	In this part of the test, I'm going to give each of you three pictures. I'd like you to talk about them on your own for about a minute, and also to answer a question briefly about your partner's pictures.
	(Candidate A), it's your turn first. Here are your pictures. They show **people who are happy for different reasons.**
	Indicate the pictures on page C10 to the candidates.
	I'd like you to compare two of the pictures, and say why the people might be feeling happy, and how memorable these occasions might be.
	All right?
Candidate A:	[*1 minute*]
Interlocutor:	Thank you.
	(Candidate B), in which picture do you think the people seem the happiest?
Candidate B:	[*Approximately 30 seconds*]
Interlocutor:	Thank you.
	Now, *(Candidate B)*, here are your pictures. They show **people doing things together.**
	Indicate the pictures on page C11 to the candidates.
	I'd like you to compare two of the pictures, and say why the people might have chosen to do these activities together, and what skills they need.
	All right?
Candidate B:	[*1 minute*]
Interlocutor:	Thank you.
	(Candidate A), which of these activities do you think would require the most preparation?
Candidate A:	[*Approximately 30 seconds*]
Interlocutor:	Thank you.

Parts 3 and 4   8 minutes (12 minutes for groups of three)

Working in the media

Part 3

Interlocutor:	Now, I'd like you to talk about something together for about three minutes. *(5 minutes for groups of three)*
	Here are some pictures showing people who work in the media.
	Indicate the pictures on page C12 to the candidates.
	First, talk to each other about what skills people might need to do these different jobs in the media. Then decide which job would be the most, and which the least, challenging.
	All right?
Candidates:	[*3 minutes (5 minutes for groups of three)*]
Interlocutor:	Thank you.

Part 4

Interlocutor:	*Select any of the following questions as appropriate:*

- What attracts people to work in the media?
- Some media personalities become very famous. What problems can this bring?
- What are the advantages and disadvantages of having a large number of television channels to choose from?
- The news is now available 24 hours a day. Do you think this is a good thing? ...... (Why?/Why not?)
- Some people say satellite television has led to a loss of national identity. What's your view?

Select any of the following prompts as appropriate:

- What do you think?
- Do you agree?
- How about you?

Thank you. That is the end of the test.

Marks and results

Paper 1   Reading

Candidates record their answers in pencil on a separate answer sheet. Two marks are given for each correct answer in **Parts 1, 2** and **3** and one mark is given for each correct answer in **Part 4**. The total score is then weighted to 40 marks for the whole Reading paper.

Paper 2   Writing

General impression mark scheme

A General Impression Mark Scheme is used in conjunction with a Task-specific Mark Scheme, which focuses on criteria specific to each particular task. The General Impression Mark Scheme summarises the content, organisation and cohesion, range of structures and vocabulary, register and format, and target reader indicated in each task.

   A summary of the General Impression Mark Scheme is given below. Trained examiners, who are co-ordinated prior to each examination session, work with a more detailed version, which is subject to updating. The CAE General Impression Mark Scheme is interpreted at Council of Europe, Common European Framework Level C1.

   * Candidates who do not address all the content points will be penalised for dealing inadequately with the requirements of the task. Candidates who fully satisfy the **Band 3** descriptor are likely to demonstrate an adequate performance at CAE level.

Band 5	For a **Band 5** to be awarded, the candidate's writing has a very positive effect on the target reader. The content is relevant* and the topic is fully developed. Information and ideas are skilfully organised through a range of cohesive devices, which are used to good effect. A wide range of complex structures and vocabulary is used effectively. Errors are minimal, and inaccuracies which do occur have no impact on communication. Register and format are consistently appropriate to the purpose of the task and the audience.
Band 4	For a **Band 4** to be awarded, the candidate's writing has a positive effect on the target reader. The content is relevant* and the topic is developed. Information and ideas are clearly organised through the use of a variety of cohesive devices. A good range of complex structures and vocabulary is used. Some errors may occur with vocabulary and when complex language is attempted, but these do not cause difficulty for the reader. Register and format are usually appropriate to the purpose of the task and the audience.
Band 3	For a **Band 3** to be awarded, the candidate's writing has a satisfactory effect on the target reader. The content is relevant* with some development of the topic. Information and ideas are generally organised logically, though cohesive devices may not always be used appropriately. A satisfactory range of structures and vocabulary is used, though word choice may lack precision. Errors which do occur do not cause difficulty for the reader. Register and format are reasonably appropriate to the purpose of the task and the audience.
Band 2	For a **Band 2** to be awarded, the candidate's writing has a negative effect on the target reader. The content is not always relevant. Information and ideas are inadequately organised and sometimes incoherent, with inaccurate use of cohesive devices. The range of structures and vocabulary is limited and/or repetitive, and errors may be basic or cause difficulty for the reader. Register and format are sometimes inappropriate to the purpose of the task and the audience.
Band 1	For a **Band 1** to be awarded, the candidate's writing has a very negative effect on the target reader. The content is often irrelevant. Information and ideas are poorly organised and often incoherent and there is minimal use of cohesive devices. The range of structures and vocabulary is severely limited, and errors frequently cause considerable difficulty for the reader. Register and format are often inappropriate to the purpose of the task and the audience.
Band 0	For a **Band zero** to be awarded, there is either too little language for assessment or the candidate's writing is totally irrelevant or illegible.

Paper 2 sample answers and examiner's comments

Sample A (Test 1, Question 1 – Letter).

Dear Tom,

Sorry for not answering your previous letter before but I've been very busy with university.

About the computer courses you ask me to recommend you, I've been searching info in the internet and I found two that seems to look what you are looking for.

The first one is called The Computer Centre. It is a very well known institute in England. You told me that you wanted to learn quickly and this centre has short as well as long courses. Also if you don't want to waste time in a big group you can have individual tuition.

The other one in the IT Training Centre. Which has special courses designed to your own needs. There are courses for beginners to advanced users. and if you are worried about the money this one has special discounts for students.

If you want my opinion about the computer courses I think The Computer Centre would be the most apropiate to your needs. You would have the posibility to have individual tuition in a short course in an unbelievable value computer centre.

Please send kisses to your sister.

I'm looking forward to hearing from you soon.

Comments

Content (points covered)
All content points addressed but not much expansion.

Organisation and cohesion
Clearly organised into paragraphs. Poor use of linkers.

Range
Some attempt at range, marred by error.

Accuracy
Several basic or impeding errors (e.g. *I found two that seems to look what you are looking for*).

Appropriacy of register and format
Appropriate.

Target reader
Would be informed.

Band 2

Sample B (Test 1, Question 3 – Competition Entry)

TO: INTERNATIONAL MAGAZINE.
COMPETITION TASK. *"Three things for the future."*
from: JULIA

The very first item I'd include in the capsule is a pack with lots of seeds, all kind of plants that I could possibly gather. The reason why I'd send those for the future is because the humanity is just about to lose the nature, destroing forests, hunting animals and fish, killing them, ruinning rivers and polluting the air and destroing the ozone camade. So, the idea is to give them – the men of the future – the opportunity to replant trees and plants, minimizing the effects of the mess we have been doing in this generation (the present).

The second thing is a tape, which contents shows all the wars we had in the past and all the conflicts we still have and the attomic bomb that made Yroshima desapear from the earth. Also the racism against any religion or color or diferences between nations. Perhaps they could learn with our mistakes and promote the peace and the justice and equality for every single man, giving children the right of been born and to grow up with dignity. Later to give the old man the well deserved rest and the fair place in the society.

Finally a picture of every race, at least to gather in a picture one face from every continent of this planet. Hopefully it would show them how equal we are and rise a felling of love and care among people and aproach human been from each other. Help them see how good the future can be and that depends on them. Happyness and peace are built by those hands that aim to promote, keep and reassure others lives. That is not easy, but on the other hand it's possible and it worth it.

Even if I don't win this competition I'm happy because I could express myself and whoever read my letter will have a chance to think about it all.

Comments

Content (points covered)
All points addressed.

Organisation and cohesion
Clearly paragraphed, but lacks clear introduction.

Range
Some attempt at range but marred by error.

Accuracy
Some impeding errors (e.g. *destroing the ozone camade, aproach human been from each other*).

Appropriacy of register and format
Appropriate.

Target reader
Would be slightly confused.

Band 2

Sample C (Test 2, Question 1 – Report)

REPORT: Holidays 01.07 – 31.07.2006

To: Tim Allsop, Manager of the International Holiday Centre

From: Alex and Jean

<u>Intro</u>

First of all, we would like to thank you for giving us the opportunity to write about our experience from last summer holidays. As requested, here is the report in which we have tried to summarize all aspects related to:

1. our work with children
2. public
3. organisation
4. food and accomodation

1. Being with children and organizing activities for them really was a fantastic experience for both of us. We really enjoyed preparing the 5 days trip to Milan and the excursion to Yvoire and were very happy to see how children were motivated by learning architecture, history, etc. Furthermore, we managed to organize lots of activities in the evenings such as games, dance shows, theathre plays, etc which captured the children's attention.

2. We were expecting to meet people from other countries and were a bit disappointed to realize that we were all from Switzerland. We think that it would be fantastic if you could manage to bring people from all nationalities for the holidays.

3. We suggest that you give clearer information in advance in order to allow assistants to prepare themselves for their jobs. For example it's important to know in advance what kind of activities you are going to teach (swimming, painting)

4. We are sorry to have to report that many children and colleagues have complained about the food and think that a particular effort should be made on accomodation, esp. cleanliness.

<u>Concl.</u> All in all, we would like to tell you once again how happy we were to work in your holiday centre and we have no doubt that the following summer holiday will be better as we have learned lots from this first experience. Looking forward to working together again next year.

Comments

Content (points covered)
All points covered with good expansion.

Organisation and cohesion
Well-organised but slightly over-length.

Range
Ambitious range of vocabulary and structure and natural language.

Accuracy
Accurate even when more complex language attempted.

Appropriacy of register and format
Appropriate.

Target reader
Would be informed.

Band 5

Sample D (Test 2, Question 4 – Information Sheet)

Do more sport!

It is common knowledge that sport is healthy and that everybody needs a break from time to time! Why not taking up a new sport or participating in one of the recreational activities our college provides?

The gym for example is open for everybody. For those who never trained I recommend a lesson with a sports teacher, which is for free. But there are so many other possibilities. If you like swimming you can either go to the pool on your own, with some friends, or take part in the swim-training to make it more professional. There are also some squash courts inside and some tennis courts outside. A possibility for everyone who likes running after a ball. You can book tennis-lessons at the sport secretary. For everyone who would like to take up a martial art to train his reflexes and his general condition there are three possibilities: Judo, Karate and Kung-Fu. Trainings are three times a week for every martial art. You can get further information about the timetables at the sport secretary. Everybody who likes football, basketball or hockey can sign in for the training on the Internet.

This October starts a new set of winter-sports which our college provides together with the iceskating and curling centre 'ISCC' about five minutes on foot from here. You can participate in the ice-skating program or take up a sport the most of you have never heard of: curling.

For all the skiers and snowboarders of you: there is some further information about snowboard and ski weekends on the internet.

Good luck with your new sport!

Comments

Content (points covered)
All points covered.

Organisation and cohesion
Satisfactory organisation.

Range
Adequate.

Accuracy
Some non-impeding errors (e.g. *why not taking*).

Appropriacy of register and format
Consistently appropriate.

Target reader
Would be informed.

Band 3

Sample E (Test 3, Question 1 – Report)

An exciting tour and learning

I am very happy to describe about my sightseeing trip to famous towns in Britain coupled with my language learning. It is a most enjoyable holiday activity I've ever taken. The tour even though lasted for a week, but it taught me a lot of history, architecture and culture of ancient and modern Britain.

It is a perfect setting for learning the language leisurely but at varied pace. The journies are comfortable and relaxing as we travelled to famous towns through a luxurious coach. It has quite exciting features for better viewing of the scenic beauty as we criss-crossed the country. The staffs are extremely friendly and helpful.

The tour is meticulously planned and co-ordinated well by the agencies and people involved in it. The guide who took us around explained with facts and figures history and background of famous buildings and places. It is never boring as he is always humorous even when explaining about dull things.

The teacher who taught us the language is an excellent communicator. He used his versatile skills and innovative teaching methods to make the learning more enjoyable and lively. We had various other activities like guided walks around the hills and famous trails. We could buy some useful stuff and memobarable things in our shopping trips. Even though we had a tiring day through our travel, learning and various other activities, the hotel stay is most comfortable and enjoyable one.

Comments

Content (points covered)
All points addressed with some expansion.

Organisation and cohesion
Organised in paragraphs but would have benefited from headings. Slightly over-length.

Range
A reasonable range.

Accuracy
Some basic errors, e.g. *It is never boring* and *It has quite exciting features for better viewing . . .*

Appropriacy of register and format
Generally appropriate.

Target reader
Would be informed.

Band 3

Sample F (Test 3, Question 5a – Essay)

> *Some different relationships between parents and children are described by the author of Big Stone Gap. I want to discuss about the relations firstly between Ave Maria and her mother and secondly between Ave Maria and her father.*
>
> *Ave Maria's mother was dead just before the beginning of the book. She born in Italy and it is obvious Ave Maria loved her and had respect for her. Ave Maria's father was dead thirteen years earlier and Ave Maria had more difficult relationship with him. She wanted his love but he never gave her attention and she often was crying about this. Ave Maria's mother wrote her a letter which the lawer gave her only after her mother's death. In the letter she explained that Ave Maria's father was not her true father. Her true father was Italian man and Ave Maria's mother must leave Italy when she got a baby. Subsequently she went to America and got married with Fred Mulligan who brought Ave Maria up as his own daughter. The letter helped Ave Maria to understand her mother and to respect her even more. It also helped her to understand Fred Mulligan and to know why did he seem cold to her.*
>
> *The strength of the relationship between Ave Maria and her mother was that they had much love for each other. The strength of the relationship between Ave Maria and her father was that he had a big sense of duty towards her even if he could not show her the love she wanted. However, the weakness in both the relationships was that they were both based on a lie. I think the relationships would have been improved if Ave Maria's mother and father would have told her the true from the start.*

Comments

Content (points covered)
The essay summarises the strengths and weaknesses of two parent-child relationships in Big Stone Gap and explains in an adequate if rather general way how these relationships could have been improved.

Organisation and cohesion
The essay is clearly organised into distinct paragraphs. There is some appropriate use of linking expressions (*firstly, secondly, subsequently, however,* etc).

Range
There is some evidence of range through the use of appropriate collocations such as *difficult relationship, sense of duty, based on a lie, tell the truth.* The candidate demonstrates a satisfactory ability to use the language of description, explanation and opinion.

Accuracy
There are a number of mistakes (such as *born* instead of *was born, get married with* instead of *get married to, was dead* instead of *died, was crying* instead of *used to cry, would have told* instead of *had told*). Although a CAE candidate should be able to use such language accurately, none of the errors interfere with communication.

Appropriacy of register and format
The register is appropriately neutral in a consistent way.

Target reader
The target reader would be informed about the writer's opinion of these two relationships.

Band 4

Sample G (Test 4, Question 2 – Article)

> *Our life is dominated by the mobile phones. They're everywhere. 'Ring, ring' has become a part of us. You can't hide yourself, because they will get you. People tend more to leave their wallet at home than this little toy, which is a miracle of modern technology.*
>
> *As most of our electronic equipments, the mobile phone has changed its design and its influence on our society very quickly. I remembered the time, when just the minority of the people had had one and the reason, why they had need it, was completely different. They spent a respectable amount of money and the service was limited. We made a distinction between personal and business use, because the first one wasn't very common.*
>
> *But nowadays, it is a basic tool like television and everyone in the Western World has access to it. We like to chat with friends, want to be everytime and everywhere, even in the bed being reachable. Honestly, it can be really practical, when you're late and tell it to your friends. Business people might phone home, while they're on a meeting in another city. As a result we can communicate in our complex world, efficiently and quickly.*
>
> *But, what is the strongest impact? Why do I see children of an age of ten years, writing messages rather than playing with friends? Are we too lazy and want only machines controlling our lifes? I do not hope so. Obviously there are many advantages, like saving time, fast connection and also being reachable, but on the whole: Personal contact is replaced by a new form of exchange. Then we express feelings, emotions and opinions through a machine, which reduces the miracle of the human being.*

Comments

Content (points covered)
All points addressed.

Organisation and cohesion
Organised into paragraphs, some attempt at linking.

Range
Ambitious attempt.

Accuracy
A number of non-impeding errors (e.g. *electronic equipments, a respectable amount of money,* and *why they had need*).

Appropriacy of register and format
Consistent.

Target reader
Would be informed.

Band 3

Sample H (Test 4, Question 3 – Proposal)

To: The Organising Committee
Subject: A suitable venue for the sports event next year.

Introduction
The purpose of this proposal is to provide information about 'YOKOHAMA' that seems to be an ideal place to hold the sports event next year. There are wide range of accommodation, transport and entertainment for visitors.

Accommodation
'YOKOHAMA' is one of the biggest port cities in Japan. Numerous holidaymakers come and stay to enjoy the special atmosphere every year. They can choose appropriate accommodation according to their tastes or budgets from youth hostels to five-star hotels.

Transport
'YOKOHAMA' is a huge city and developed well, so several means of transportation are provided – such as tubes, trains, buses and rent-a-cars. Generally, the public transport system in Japan is very reliable. They always run punctually. In addition, the nearest international air port is 45 minutes away by bus. The only question is conjestion in rush hours, more specifically from 8.00am to 10.00am in the morning, but this could be sorted out by some regulations during the events.

Entertainment
'YOKOHAMA' is not only a modern city, but also a historical city. This means the city could attract anyone who have their own interests. The city use to be a capital city of Japan in 13th century so some temples built at that time still stand there. They are worth visiting. On the other hand, modern facilities – an exciting amusement park, a Marine Museum, a zoo and an art museum – are there. Should someone feel tired during their stay, she/he could ramble in a park on a hill looking onto the Tokyo Bay. Moreover, YOKOHAMA is next to Tokyo, a capital city of Japan. So, people could go there in half an hour by train and enjoy visiting touristic sites in Tokyo, shopping and arts – such as theatres in Japanese traditional style or modern, concerts and so on.

Conclusion
All in all, I have no hesitation in recommending 'YOKOHAMA' for the place where the next sports event will be held. There are no better places than YOKOHAMA, considering its excellent accommodation transport and entertainment.

Comments

Contents (points covered)
All points covered. Good realisation of task.

Organisation and cohesion
Attention paid to organisation and cohesion with appropriate headings. Effective introduction and conclusion.

Range
Evidence of range of vocabulary (e.g. *according to their tastes or budgets*) and structure (e.g. *I have no hesitation in recommending* and *45 minutes away by bus*).

Accuracy
Sufficiently natural but with occasional minor slips (e.g. *The city use to be* and *anyone who have their own interests*) and problems with articles (e.g. *a capital city*). In places generally accurate even when more complex language attempted.

Appropriacy of register and format
Appropriate.

Target reader
Positive effect. Target reader would be informed, and would consider the proposal.

Band 4

Paper 3   Use of English

One mark is given for each correct answer in **Parts 1, 2** and **3**. Two marks are given for each correct answer in **Part 4**. For **Part 5**, candidates are awarded a mark of 2, 1 or 0 for each question according to the accuracy of their response. Correct spelling is required in **Parts 2, 3, 4** and **5**. The total mark is subsequently weighted to 40.

Paper 4   Listening

One mark is given for each correct answer. The total is weighted to give a mark out of 40 for the paper.

For security reasons, several versions of the Listening paper are used at each administration of the examination. Before grading, the performance of the candidates in each of the versions is compared and marks adjusted to compensate for any imbalance in levels of difficulty.

Paper 5   Speaking

Candidates are assessed on their own individual performance and not in relation to each other, according to the following five analytical criteria: grammatical resource, vocabulary resource, discourse management, pronunciation and interactive communication. Assessment is based on performance in the whole test and not in particular parts of the test.

Both examiners assess the candidates. The assessor applies detailed analytical scales, and the interlocutor applies a global achievement scale, which is based on the analytical scales.

Analytical scales

Grammatical resource

This refers to the accurate and appropriate use of a range of both simple and complex forms. Performance is viewed in terms of the overall effectiveness of the language used in spoken interaction.

Vocabulary resource

This refers to the candidate's ability to use a wide range of vocabulary to meet task requirements. At CAE level, the tasks require candidates to speculate and exchange views on unfamiliar topics. Performance is viewed in terms of the overall effectiveness of the language used in spoken interaction.

Discourse management

This refers to the candidate's ability to link utterances together to form coherent speech, without undue hesitation. The utterances should be relevant to the tasks and should be arranged logically to develop the themes or arguments required by the tasks.

Pronunciation

This refers to the candidate's ability to produce intelligible utterances to fulfil the task requirements. This includes stress and intonation as well as individual sounds. Examiners put themselves in the position of the non-ESOL specialist and assess the overall impact of the pronunciation and the degree of effort required to understand the candidate.

Interactive communication

This refers to the candidate's ability to take an active part in the development of the discourse. This requires the ability to participate in the range of interactive situations in the test and to develop discussions on a range of topics by initiating and responding appropriately. This also refers to the deployment of strategies to maintain interaction at an appropriate level throughout the test so that the tasks can be fulfilled.

Global achievement

This refers to the candidate's overall effectiveness in dealing with the tasks in the four separate parts of the CAE Speaking test. The global mark is an independent, impression mark which reflects the assessment of the candidate's performance from the interlocutor's perspective.

Marks

Marks for each of the criteria are awarded out of a nine-point scale. Marks for the Speaking test are subsequently weighted to produce a final mark out of 40.

CAE typical minimum adequate performance

The candidate develops the interaction with contributions which are mostly coherent and extended when dealing with the CAE level tasks. Grammar is mostly accurate and vocabulary appropriate. Utterances are understood with very little strain on the listener.

Test 1 Key

Paper 1   Reading (1 hour 15 minutes)

Part 1

1 C   2 B   3 D   4 A   5 B   6 D

Part 2

7 F   8 A   9 G   10 B   11 D   12 C

Part 3

13 B   14 D   15 D   16 A   17 D   18 C   19 B

Part 4

20 A   21 B   22 D   23 D   24 B   25 C   26 B   27 A   28 E
29 D   30 A   31 B   32 A   33 E   34 D

Paper 2   Writing (1 hour 30 minutes)

Task-specific Mark Schemes

Part 1

Question 1

Content (points covered)
For Band 3 or above, the candidate's **letter** must:
- outline the advantages of each centre
- say which one you recommend
- explain why

Organisation and cohesion
Clearly organised into paragraphs with appropriate linking devices.
Letter format with suitable opening and closing formulae.
Early reference to reason for writing.

Range
Language of description, evaluation and justification.
Vocabulary related to computers and study.

Appropriacy of register and format
Informal to unmarked. Must be consistent.

Target reader
Would be informed.

Part 2

Question 2

Content (points covered)
For Band 3 or above, the candidate's **article** must:
• state which two sports they most enjoy watching
• give reasons for their choices
• state whether they think sports in their country have been influenced by sports from abroad
• give reasons.

Organisation and cohesion
Clearly organised into paragraphs with appropriate linking devices.

Range
Language of description, opinion and justification.

Appropriacy of register and format
May mix registers if appropriate to approach taken by candidate.

Target reader
Would be informed.

Question 3

Content (points covered)
For Band 3 or above, the candidate's **competition entry** must:
• recommend three items to put in a time capsule
• explain why these items would be of interest in the future.

Organisation and cohesion
Clearly organised into paragraphs with appropriate linking devices.

Range
Language of description, recommendation and explanation.

Appropriacy of register and format
May mix registers if appropriate to approach taken by candidate.

Target reader
Would consider the entry.

Question 4

Content (points covered)
For Band 3 or above, the candidate's **report** must:
• outline strengths and weaknesses of education in their country
• suggest at least **one** future development.

Organisation and cohesion
Clearly organised into paragraphs with appropriate linking devices.
Headings may be an advantage.
N.B. Letter format acceptable.

Range
Language of description, opinion and suggestion.
Vocabulary related to education.

Appropriacy of register and format
Unmarked to formal. Must be consistent.

Target reader
Would be informed.

Question 5 (a)

Content (points covered)
For Band 3 or above, the candidate's **review** must:
• discuss aspects of the story which would be most interesting for people from the candidate's country
• give reasons for the candidate's opinions
• encourage the target reader to read / watch *Big Stone Gap*.

Organisation and cohesion
Clearly organised into paragraphs with appropriate linking devices.

Range
Language of description, opinion, explanation and persuasion.
Vocabulary related to description of and comment on a book.

Appropriacy of register and format
May mix registers if appropriate to approach taken by candidate.

Target reader
Would be informed.

Question 5 (b)

Content (points covered)
For Band 3 or above, the candidate's **essay** must:
• explain the significance of the title
• comment on how appropriate the candidate feels the title is.

Organisation and cohesion
Clearly organised into paragraphs with appropriate linking devices.

Range
Language of description, opinion and explanation.
Vocabulary related to comment on a book.

Appropriacy of register and format
May mix registers if appropriate to approach taken by candidate.

Target reader
Would be informed.

Paper 3   Use of English (1 hour)

Part 1

1 C   2 A   3 D   4 B   5 C   6 A   7 D   8 C
9 A   10 B   11 D   12 D

Part 2

13 our   14 in / during   15 which / that   16 be   17 instead   18 means
19 who   20 themselves   21 have   22 at   23 how / where   24 us
25 this/that   26 as   27 the

Part 3

28 lookout   29 invasion   30 eagerness   31 glorious   32 talking   33 intensity
34 dependent   35 increasingly   36 unlike   37 seasonal / seasonable

Part 4

38 sense   39 move   40 fair   41 missed   42 terms

Part 5

43 price of petrol has risen | sharply   44 on the point | of leaving   45 not | so successful
46 led to | the cancellation / cancelling   47 far as | computer games are concerned
48 high time | Carlos got / had   49 with a / any chance | of winning   50 made a great / big
(etc.) impression | on

Paper 4   Listening (approximately 40 minutes)

Part 1

1 B   2 C   3 C   4 A   5 B   6 A

Part 2

7 international   8 land(-)owners   9 championship   10 cities   11 (urban) parks
12 grow quickly / fast   13 nature reserves   14 (local) community

Part 3

15 A   16 A   17 C   18 D   19 B   20 C

Part 4

21 E   22 H   23 F   24 B   25 D   26 C   27 F   28 G   29 D   30 A

Transcript   *This is the Cambridge Certificate in Advanced English Listening Test. Test One.*

I'm going to give you the instructions for this test. I'll introduce each part of the test and give you time to look at the questions.

At the start of each piece you'll hear this sound:

tone

You'll hear each piece twice.

*Remember, while you're listening, write your answers on the **question paper**. You'll have **five minutes** at the end of the test to **copy your answers onto the separate answer sheet**.*

There'll now be a pause. Please ask any questions now, because you must not speak during the test.

[pause]

PART 1   *Now open your question paper and look at Part One.*

[pause]

You'll hear three different extracts. For questions one to six, choose the answer (A, B or C) which fits best according to what you hear. There are two questions for each extract.

Extract 1	*You overhear two friends discussing a documentary film about the sea. Now look at questions one and two.*

[pause]

tone

Woman:	I thought it was a great film – so visually exciting – and the sharks looked really scary at times.
Man:	I hate to admit it but it made me jump a bit at times too – I guess recent advances in camera technology helped. But that commentary – really irritating and patronising.
Woman:	Really? But didn't you recognise the voices? It was J.D. Stone and Kate Donohue – you normally like them.
Man:	Huh. Well, I also didn't take kindly to being lectured by them about the environment. I mean I'm against global warming and all that business, don't get me wrong, but this message they were giving out just seemed tacked on to me.
Woman:	But think how inspiring it was for the young kids in the audience, and at least it wasn't a carbon copy of all those other marine films – you know like *Deep Blue* and *Blue Planet*.
Man:	Um, but I guess there's an audience for them or they wouldn't make them, would they? But one amazing thing – did you know it takes two hours underwater for each three minutes of film? Can you imagine?

[pause]

tone

Now you'll hear the recording again.

[The recording is repeated.]

[pause]

Extract 2	*You hear part of a radio interview with a man called Gerald Barton who has travelled extensively. Now look at questions three and four.*

[pause]

tone

Interviewer:	Now Gerald, I understand you 'collect' countries, ones you've visited – and make it all the more interesting by crossing them off an alphabetical list. What's the tally so far?
Gerald:	Well, I haven't been to every country. It's 64 I believe, and that includes every letter except X. I work for a very understanding computer firm which lets me take weeks off at a time. I'd say their tolerance probably deserves public recognition! And like a lot of other travellers I've met, I have a website where I keep an up-to-date list – I checked my figures this morning.
Interviewer:	And how do you decide when a country can be added to your list?
Gerald:	Well, it doesn't count if I whizz through on a train, or change planes at the airport. My girlfriend says I have to spend at least one night in the country – but I'm making the rules, so it's up to me. I reckon it's got to be something positive – like going to a famous building or seeing a particular natural feature. Of course what I'm aiming at is getting a feel of the place, so I talk to people as often as I can.

[pause]

tone

Now you'll hear the recording again.

[The recording is repeated.]

[pause]

Extract 3   *You hear part of a radio interview with Sarah Grey, who writes and illustrates children's books. Now look at questions five and six.*

[pause]

tone

Interviewer: Sarah, I've been carrying round one of your books in preparation for this interview, and I've been amazed – a woman saw me with it in a posh restaurant and said, 'Oh, I loved that book'. And there was a three-year-old on the tube, just as enthusiastic. What explains the appeal, do you think?

Sarah: It's difficult to say, but I find the same when I attend book events. Everyone remembers Freddie. I think it's simply because they know what he looks like from the illustrations. It's nice to encounter interesting characters – and in children's books they often have magic powers, and they go off on quite amazing adventures.

Interviewer: So what about television? That's visual.

Sarah: Well, children are bombarded with images on screen from the cradle. That's just a fact of modern life we've all come to accept. Sometimes I think it gives them almost too much for the imagination to play with. There's not much chance for them to take in detail, slow down and make a leisurely exploration of a story. There's a kind of visual overload – and some of it is very strident – noisy and garish.

[pause]

tone

Now you'll hear the recording again.

[The recording is repeated.]

[pause]

That's the end of Part One.
Now turn to Part Two.

[pause]

PART 2   *Part Two*

You'll hear a man called Tom Trueman giving a lecture about golf courses and the environment. For questions 7 to 14, complete the sentences. You now have 45 seconds to look at Part Two.

[pause]

tone

Lecturer: Good afternoon. I'm here to talk about the rather delicate question of golf courses in the countryside. I want to look at the growth of golf in this country and make some suggestions regarding its future development.

A few years ago, a report was published by the body that governs the sport nationally. At that time, the popularity of golf was expanding rapidly on the back of all the publicity surrounding the success of certain local golfers in international competitions.

The report said that people who didn't belong to existing golf clubs, but who wanted to start playing the game, found there simply weren't enough facilities to go round. So, the report concluded, around 700 courses would have to be built to meet the demand.

Following that report, there was, as you can imagine, enormous interest amongst landowners, not to mention businessmen, who suddenly realised that there was money to be made out of golf. Now, the ordinary beginner couldn't really afford to pay for a high standard of facilities, but, for some reason, developers tended to build championship golf courses, so that quite a few of the hundreds built across the country failed financially.

And, of course, not everybody likes golf courses anyway. They cause changes to the local environment and are used only by those with money, and that often means people driving out from the cities, rather than the local population.

A further objection to golf courses is that, although they don't involve much building, the smooth close-cut grass gives them the ordered appearance of urban parks, because developers seem to be obsessed with the idea of stripping everything out and starting again. The land is levelled out, then artificial bumps are introduced, alien species of plants, often imported from abroad, are put in; trees that grow fast are particularly popular, as are new varieties of grass that provide a good walking surface. And, of course, this means that wild animals and other forms of native wildlife are uprooted and suffer as a result.

But my point is why should all this destruction be necessary? Why do all golf courses have to look the same? I believe that, with a little bit of imagination, many courses could easily be turned into nature reserves, where interesting or rare plant varieties could be preserved. Many of the arguments raised by the critics would be answered in this way and I think this is an approach that should be considered before any more golf courses are built in this country. Most importantly, courses should be designed to attract rather than drive away wildlife. A knock-on effect of this would be another layer of use, as schoolchildren and others could come to study the natural habitats that would be preserved, making the golf course much more an integral part of the local community as well as the local ecology.

So, what work can we do . . .?

[pause]

tone

Now you'll hear the recording again.

[The recording is repeated.]

[pause]

That's the end of Part Two.
Now turn to Part Three.

[pause]

PART 3   *Part Three*

You'll hear part of an interview with two chefs, Jane and Chris, who both won prizes in the National Railway Chef of the Year competition. For questions 15 to 20, choose the answer (A, B, C or D) which fits best according to what you hear. You now have one minute to look at Part Three.

[pause]

tone

Greg:	Serving more than 200,000 meals a year would be a challenge for any chef, but step up constraints of time, space and a demand for culinary excellence and you have the life of a railway chef. Chris and Jane, the idea of having to cook in cramped surroundings, with limited ingredients and a very tight schedule, as you did in the recent competition, must have been a terrifying prospect . . .
Chris:	Well, hardly – I actually operate under those restrictions every day!
Jane:	That's true, of course, we both do – but there's always the added danger that things can go wrong, and the challenge of preparing a top-quality, three-course meal for four – which costs no more than £50 – and in front of all those judges!
Greg:	Well, Jane, you were a runner up and Chris came first. I gather you faced some stiff competition from the other finalists.
Jane:	No doubt about that. All the chefs who entered the competition were brilliant in their own way – but someone has to win! But the real problem is trying to be creative as the train hurtles through the countryside at over 100 miles an hour – there's little room for mistakes – and you have to be able to keep your balance!
Chris:	Actually, I'd only been a railway chef for three months. And I can tell you that life on board is no easy ride. There's no nipping out to get the extra bunch of parsley, or a lemon.
Greg:	But you're used to working under pressure all the same, aren't you? How do you set about being organised?
Chris:	You've just got to make sure you're focused on the job. Being able to keep an eye on a dozen things at once is also an advantage!
Greg:	But do you actually enjoy what you're doing?
Jane:	There's plenty of scope to express yourself as a chef in the job – and the open kitchen means that customers will often compliment you personally on the food. That's one of the biggest highlights of the job.
Chris:	I'd certainly go along with that. Very few restaurant chefs have the chance to experience that.
Greg:	And what about the menus, who decides what to cook?
Jane:	They're decided in advance for the whole railway network by two extremely famous chefs, who are actually brothers. I suppose we both find it restricting.
Chris:	Hmm. I do get a bit frustrated from time to time – think I could be a little more adventurous – but it's all a question of adaptability – which I suspect Jane is better at than I am!
Jane:	Not at all – I can be quite inflexible when the mood takes me!
Greg:	So what would be a typical routine for you both?
Chris:	You have to start at around 5.30 in the morning – check that all the ingredients have been delivered – then it's a mad rush to get everything ready.
Jane:	And precious little time to rest any other time during the day, as you often have to set tables on other trains and help other staff. Timing's particularly tight, you see. In other restaurants orders come in and go out over two or three hours, but we have to turn round before the passengers reach their stations. It's all a bit nerve-racking.

Greg:	So what motivated you to do this in the first place?
Chris:	I've been on the move ever since I left college. So when I got engaged, I decided it was time to settle down. So when I saw this job, it seemed a reasonable compromise between personal commitments and my reluctance to stay in one place.
Jane:	For me it was something that just caught my eye – not just ordinary run-of-the-mill stuff. And, if you get the time, you get a good view out of the windows!
Greg:	And how do you stop things from spilling over when the train moves?
Chris:	It's not a problem for me. I was a chef on a liner, so I've got plenty of experience of cookery in motion!
Jane:	Yes, but I think it helps if you only half fill saucepans with boiling water – even so, they often spill over and you start saying nasty things to yourself about the driver – and it's not usually his fault!
Chris:	Let's just say that you quickly learn not to put things under the grill without keeping an eye on them!
Greg:	Has either of you had any major disasters?
Chris:	[*laughs*] I'd only been in the job for three days and I had this huge roast in the oven. I opened the door, turned around for a moment, distracted, I suppose, and it just flew out. Fortunately it landed in the sink, so it was okay.
Greg:	And what qualities would you say it was necessary for a railway chef to have?
Jane:	From my point of view, dedication and determination – you won't get anywhere without these!
Chris:	And, let's admit it – a sense of humour. There have been times when I would have resigned long ago if I hadn't had that!

[pause]

tone

Now you'll hear the recording again.

[The recording is repeated.]

[pause]

That's the end of Part Three.
Now turn to Part Four.

[pause]

PART 4

Part Four

Part Four consists of two tasks. You'll hear five short extracts in which people are talking about their future retirement. Look at Task One. For questions 21 to 25, choose from the list A to H each speaker's present occupation. Now look at Task Two. For questions 26 to 30, choose from the list A to H what each speaker is looking forward to doing when they retire. While you listen you must complete both tasks. You now have 45 seconds to look at Part Four.

[pause]

tone

Speaker One: Work has involved so much of my life from first training to be an attorney in my twenties. I wanted to help people by fighting injustice and found myself dealing with endless paperwork for house sales instead. So I decided to use my skills in a different way and taught law. It took a while to adapt but I love the contact with young people. I'll miss that, but there'll be compensations. Everyone says I'll enjoy staying in bed longer, but I'm at my best in the early morning so that's out. I've spent ages sitting reading textbooks and assignments so it'll be good to be more active – might even get a dog!

[pause]

Speaker Two: I'm looking forward to retiring – living without the pressure of constant deadlines and the hassle of airports. Visiting faraway places sounds wonderful, but the ones I see are usually in crisis and anyway my time's devoted to getting interviews rather than sightseeing. Perhaps if I'd followed my original idea of studying architecture, life might have been less hectic. What to do with all the extra time is the question. I should do something energetic like growing vegetables or cycling but the outdoors isn't my scene. Strangely, although I've spent my life producing the printed word, it'll be great to settle down with other people's – biographies, fiction and so on.

[pause]

Speaker Three: I'm retiring early, not because of my health – in fact the medical profession must love me because I hardly ever consult them! There are just so many things I want to do. I've been talking to friends and we think it's vital to do new things, so I'm going to try my hand at watercolours – landscapes initially. My wife's learning Russian and I'd love to join her except that my lack of language skills rules it out. I'll stick with landscapes. I can enjoy being outside at the same time. I should have followed my father into agriculture really. Being away from the office and not having to work on spreadsheets all day will be great.

[pause]

Speaker Four: What am I looking forward to? Above all not working during weekends when I'd rather be at home. I've enjoyed the contact with people though. That's why I went into this profession rather than something like the law or business. The responsibility for people's well-being does weigh on you so it'll be good to lose that. I've managed to visit a lot of countries – mostly for pleasure but there were conferences on my speciality too, so I won't be jumping on the first cruise ship. It'll be nice to do more locally, especially if it means doing things with people you really like and getting to know them better.

[pause]

Speaker Five: I'm handing over to my son soon and moving to the coast. It'll be strange not having the animals around, but they were a tie. You couldn't leave them for even a day, unless somebody took over, so it'll be good to be able to explore faraway places. My son thinks I should have a garden so I can plant roses and grow vegetables. Having dealt with crops all my life, I think I'll give it a rest. My wife says I should go to college and do something different like a language or some amateur drama. She thinks I should have gone on the stage – comedy probably. Too much like hard work!

[pause]

tone

Now you'll hear the recording again.

[The recording is repeated.]

[pause]

That's the end of Part Four.

*There'll now be a pause of **five minutes** for you to **copy your answers onto the separate answer sheet**. Be sure to follow the numbering of all the questions. I'll remind you when there's one minute left, so that you're sure to finish in time.*

[Teacher, pause the recording here for five minutes. Remind your students when they have one minute left.]

That's the end of the test. Please stop now. Your supervisor will now collect all the question papers and answer sheets.

Test 2 Key

Paper 1   Reading (1 hour 15 minutes)

Part 1

1 D   2 C   3 D   4 A   5 B   6 A

Part 2

7 G   8 A   9 D   10 E   11 F   12 C

Part 3

13 B   14 D   15 C   16 B   17 D   18 D   19 C

Part 4

20 D   21 C   22 B   23 D   24 C   25 A   26 B   27 D   28 A
29 B   30 A   31 D   32 C   33 B   34 A

Paper 2   Writing (1 hour 30 minutes)

Part 1

Question 1

Content (points covered)
For Band 3 or above, the candidate's **report** must:
• outline experiences
• make suggestions for improvements.

Organisation and cohesion
Clearly organised into paragraphs with appropriate linking devices.
Numbered points may be appropriate.

Range
Language of description and suggestion.

Appropriacy of register and format
Formal to unmarked. Must be consistent.

Target reader
Would be informed.

Part 2

Question 2

Content (points covered)
For Band 3 or above, the candidate's **letter of application** must:
• describe the type(s) of music suggested for festival
• describe the candidate's own musical tastes
• suggest why the candidate should be employed as a judge.

Organisation and cohesion
Clearly organised into paragraphs with appropriate linking devices.
Letter format with suitable opening and closing formulae. Early reference to reason for writing.

Range
Language of description, explanation and recommendation.
Vocabulary related to music.

Appropriacy of register and format
Unmarked to formal. Must be consistent.

Target reader
Would be informed and consider the application.

Question 3

Content (points covered)
For Band 3 or above, the candidate's **contribution** must:
• describe at least two types of jobs and how to find them
• refer to pay and/or conditions
• give advice about possible problems.

Organisation and cohesion
Clearly organised into paragraphs with appropriate linking devices.

Range
Language of description, explanation and advice.

Appropriacy of register and format
Any, as long as consistent.

Target reader
Would be informed and would consider the contribution to the guide book.

Question 4

Content (points covered)
For Band 3 or above, the candidate's **information sheet** must:
• include information about facilities and/or activities
• point out benefits of taking up opportunities
• encourage readers to use facilities/join in activities.

Organisation and cohesion
Clearly organised into paragraphs with appropriate linking devices.
Headings would be an advantage.

Range
Vocabulary related to leisure activities.

Appropriacy of register and format
Informal to unmarked. Must be consistent.

Target reader
Would be informed.

Question 5 (a)

Content (points covered)
For Band 3 or above, the candidate's **report** must:
• explain what the candidate generally learnt about life from *Big Stone Gap*
• explain what the candidate learnt from it from a language point of view.

Organisation and cohesion
Clearly organised into paragraphs with appropriate linking devices.

Range
Language of description, opinion and explanation.
Vocabulary related to description of and comment on a book.

Appropriacy of register and format
May mix registers if appropriate to approach taken by candidate.

Target reader
Would be informed.

Question 5 (b)

Content (points covered)
For Band 3 or above, the candidate's **article** must:
- discuss the hero's behaviour
- state how the writer feels about the hero's behaviour
- explain whether the writer would have behaved in the same way in at least two of the situations in which the hero found himself.

Organisation and cohesion
Clearly organised into paragraphs with appropriate linking devices.

Range
Language of description, opinion and speculation.
Vocabulary related to character and behaviour.

Appropriacy of register and format
May mix registers if appropriate to approach taken by candidate.

Target reader
Would be informed.

Paper 3   Use of English (1 hour)

Part 1

1 A   2 C   3 D   4 A   5 B   6 B   7 D   8 D
9 B   10 C   11 C   12 A

Part 2

13 One / A   14 at   15 another   16 every / any   17 be
18 no / little   19 such   20 as   21 was   22 without   23 had
24 over / beyond / across   25 would   26 what   27 its

Part 3

28 expectations   29 Basically   30 survival   31 success   32 affordable   33 regardless
34 Simplicity   35 incapable   36 effective   37 repeatedly

Part 4

38 showed   39 point   40 take   41 clear   42 break

Part 5

43 grew / increased / went up | as a result of   44 a change | for the   45 came as | a surprise to   46 there's | no knowing   47 she was / would / 'd be interested | in going   48 haven't heard | from Georgia for / in OR have heard nothing | from Georgia for / in
49 was made | responsible   50 cost you | the / a job

Paper 4   Listening (approximately 40 minutes)

Part 1

1 C   2 B   3 A   4 C   5 B   6 B

Part 2

7 her parents / family / Helen(')s parents / family   8 remembering / memorising / learning (her / the lines) (by heart)   9 (throat) operation   10 (great) comedy (actress / actor) / comic / comedian / comedienne   11 (a) perfume(s) / scent(s)
12 letters / correspondence   13 (reading) (the) reviews   14 (her / the) audience(s)

Part 3

15 D   16 D   17 A   18 B   19 A   20 A

Part 4

21 E   22 D   23 C   24 A   25 H   26 E   27 G   28 B   29 D   30 C

Transcript   *This is the Cambridge Certificate in Advanced English, Listening Test. Test Two.*

I'm going to give you the instructions for this test. I'll introduce each part of the test and give you time to look at the questions.

At the start of each piece you'll hear this sound:

tone

You'll hear each piece twice.

*Remember, while you're listening, write your answers on the **question paper**. You'll have **five minutes** at the end of the test to **copy your answers onto the separate answer sheet**.*

There'll now be a pause. Please ask any questions now, because you must not speak during the test.

[pause]

PART 1   *Now open your question paper and look at Part One.*

[pause]

You'll hear three different extracts. For questions one to six, choose the answer (A, B or C) which fits best according to what you hear. There are two questions for each extract.

Extract 1   *You hear part of a radio discussion about the ongoing television dramas known as soap operas. Now look at questions one and two.*

[pause]

tone

Woman: My main criticism of soap operas is that there's much more emphasis now on things happening rather than on the development of character.

Man: Well, soaps, and in fact all dramas, have got to have things happening for their characters to have things to do. But over the last few years there's been a lot more competition from both domestic and imported shows. So you've got to have much bigger events so that the press pick them up and make the audience aware of what's coming and so curious to switch on.

Woman: Another thing is the way some soaps insist on putting across public 'messages' on social issues, the environment and so on, and do it with a very heavy hand, almost like a public service announcement rather than an entertainment programme.

Man: Well, I disapprove strongly of soaps handing out instructions but I think they do have an ability to give audiences information about an issue through the development of the storyline. People can see how characters deal with whatever the issue is and then they can talk about it themselves. That's got to be valuable, hasn't it?

[pause]

tone

Now you'll hear the recording again.

[The recording is repeated.]

[pause]

Extract 2   *You overhear a conversation in a shop between a jewellery-maker and a customer. Now look at questions three and four.*

[pause]

tone

Jeweller: Can I help you?

Customer: I'm trying to find a present for my wife's birthday ... Your jewellery's really beautiful – these designs must've taken you a lifetime to create.

Jeweller: Well, thank you! But I've actually only been in jewellery for a couple of years. I was a nurse and had a bad back, so I was advised to try something lighter ...

Customer: And took up jewellery.

Jeweller: Not immediately. I did an evening course in life drawing at a school of art, hard work but fun, and then when I saw some of the jewellery that students produce, I was hooked!

Customer: It must all be a total change from nursing ...

Jeweller: Well, it was a bit of a shock not having a regular pay-packet.

Customer:	. . . I've never seen anything like these exquisite glassy shapes you've incorporated into your designs.
Jeweller:	I *have* been very lucky because my work caught on straight away, so this made me sure I should continue along the same lines . . . but I still leave the *making* to the last minute. I find I do my best craft work when I'm under a bit of pressure actually.

[pause]

tone

Now you'll hear the recording again.

[The recording is repeated.]

[pause]

Extract 3

You overhear two colleagues, Richard and Kate, discussing a round-the-world trip Kate is planning to go on. Now look at questions five and six.

[pause]

tone

Richard:	So, Kate, your trip starts next week, and it's just the first bit you do on your own?
Kate:	Yeah, I'm doing a week at a language school in Paraguay and then a fortnight working in an animal conservation park.
Richard:	Why did you decide to do a language course?
Kate:	I suppose if I think about it, I want to be able to communicate with local people. And I don't know if anyone at the conservation place speaks English.
Richard:	That could be tricky! What's the Spanish for 'If I were you, I'd keep well away from that iguana'?
Kate:	That's why I need to do the course! Anyway, then I meet up with my group and move on to New Zealand.
Richard:	You've known them for ages, haven't you?
Kate:	That doesn't mean we don't have arguments though. One of them, especially, can be a real pain. But there are things that, realistically, I think I need to do in a group, like whitewater rafting, so I'll have to put up with that. Not sure they'll be able to cope with the camping though – they're used to home comforts!

[pause]

tone

Now you'll hear the recording again.

[The recording is repeated.]

[pause]

That's the end of Part One.
Now turn to Part Two.

[pause]

PART 2

Part Two

You'll hear part of a radio programme in which an expert on theatre history is talking about the life of a famous actress called Helen Perry. For questions 7 to 14, complete the sentences.

You now have 45 seconds to look at Part Two.

[pause]

tone

Presenter: We have in the studio today Vernon Hall, an expert on theatre history, to tell us all about Helen Perry, one of the greatest actresses of all time.

Vernon: Helen Perry was born in 1847, right in the middle of the nineteenth century, when the theatre was the main form of public entertainment. Her acting career didn't actually get off to a very promising start, which was not surprising given that acting was considered an unsuitable career for a young woman. So she waited until she was 22 before going on stage, to avoid her parents' disapproval.

Once on the stage, she found that she had other problems. Although her first part was very small, she had great trouble learning the lines and, according to her, this was something she found difficult throughout her acting career. However, this did not prevent her from becoming an incredibly successful actress. People who saw her act said that the thing that made her so special was her voice – apparently, it had an almost hypnotic quality. However, it nearly brought her career to an abrupt end when she was in her fifties. Her voice just got lower and huskier and she quite often lost it when she had a cold. Finally she had a very risky throat operation – which paid off, because she went on acting for another 25 years after that.

Helen Perry is now remembered as a great classical actress but she was actually very skilful. She was, for example, a great comedy actress which was what really gave her broad popular appeal. And she was immensely popular. At the height of her fame, people could buy all sorts of mementos like postcards and paperweights with her picture on. She was one of the first stars to have a perfume named in her honour, and that brand, simply called 'Helen', remained on sale until quite recently.

It's always been known that several famous plays were written for her, but what isn't so well-known is that she had literary talent herself because we have the letters she exchanged with one writer and they show she had great style and wit.

Some people feel that she should have retired earlier, when she was at her peak, but personally, I disagree. We have no film of her acting, of course, but from the reviews of her performances towards the end of her career we can see that although she had difficulty walking, she is still described as magnetic.

She picked up quite a few honorary degrees from various universities, something which had never happened to an actress before. She was pleased to get academic recognition, of course, but what *really* pleased her was the way that the audiences loved her, and that was all the recognition she really needed. She'll certainly never be forgotten.

[pause]

tone

Now you'll hear the recording again.

[The recording is repeated.]

[pause]

That's the end of Part Two.
Now turn to Part Three.

[pause]

PART 3

Part Three

You'll hear a radio interview with the writer, Tom Davies. For questions 15 to 20, choose the answer (A, B, C or D) which fits best according to what you hear. You now have one minute to look at Part Three.

[pause]

tone

Interviewer: My guest today is Tom Davies. He has written a series of highly-acclaimed novels, as well as a play and two successful film scripts. He has said, 'I love the solitude, the sheer pleasure of writing, the secret excitement.' Tom, writing is a solitary business, but does it go on being exciting?

Tom Davies: Well, writing *is* an exciting process, although there are good days and bad days, obviously. I remember when I started, I used to sweat for so long over one sentence that it really wasn't much of a pleasure. But I got past that stage and yes, I do find that when things go well, when things are working out, it *is* very absorbing.

Interviewer: But surely less secret these days, now that you've won major prizes?

Tom Davies: Possibly. I recently read out a whole chunk of my work-in-progress at a literary festival because it's one way of trying these things out, whereas in the past I'd been too frightened that if I talked about what I was writing, I would somehow lose control of it. But I think generally I don't talk about what I am intending to write, because I'm still not entirely sure myself which way it's going to go. But once something is down in a first or second draft, then you can try it out and see how it sounds.

Interviewer: And you've said that at any one time there are as many as ten or fifteen ideas for novels floating around in your head. How do you choose which one to follow up?

Tom Davies: You've got to find the idea that's got the right kind of urgency and it's not a rational decision. It's patience and luck and turning up at your desk every morning even when nothing seems to be coming. If you're not there, then nothing is precisely what will happen. But once I get started, then a good day would be two or three hundred words.

Interviewer: And then do you hone it, do you go back over it?

Tom Davies: I go back all the time until I get to the stage when I won't look at it again because you need the distance of time to look back and see it from a different perspective.

Interviewer: And is there anyone who you can then give this manuscript to and say, 'Look, before I go any further, tell me what you think of this'?

Tom Davies: I give the finished draft to certain old friends who're permitted to be as brutal as they like. That's very useful because I think there's a danger for writers as they get older, as their reputations get established, that publishers won't tell them if they've any serious doubts about a piece. So sceptical friends are very important to give you the benefit of a truthful opinion.

Interviewer: And you trust these friends?

Tom Davies:	Absolutely. The first time I tried this, years ago, a friend of mine said, 'Look, I think this novel's absolutely terrible, put it in a drawer and forget about it.' And I didn't speak to him for eighteen months. But after that I learnt that if you give someone your novel to read, you've got to allow them to say that kind of thing. These days I wouldn't take it so personally.
Interviewer:	And although you've denied any suggestion that you write about yourself, there are actually all sorts of bits and pieces of you dotted all over your work, aren't there?
Tom Davies:	Someone said that you can't write two hundred words in a novel without giving something of yourself away and I suppose that's true. Perhaps that's why I've always been a bit defensive about my work.
Interviewer:	Now, despite those two successful film scripts, you haven't, strangely, had a lot of luck translating your stories onto the big screen, have you? Why's that?
Tom Davies:	Oh well, my first experience was of a low-budget English film. And because we had so little money to work with, it was wonderfully uncomplicated and I thought, 'Oh what a brilliant life. I could write novels and then in between each one, I could do a film.'
Interviewer:	Because it's so much easier?
Tom Davies:	Well, it was such fun being away on location surrounded by fabulously competent people, all taking fierce pride in their ability to do something so well and very quickly. The panic of the ticking clock, the things going wrong and then somehow being solved at the last minute, all that was marvellous for someone who usually spends his time locked up in an empty room.
Interviewer:	So it's actually harder to write a good screenplay?
Tom Davies:	No, I wouldn't say that. Indeed, I don't think a screenplay is a literary form in itself. It's more a set of instructions, a bit like a recipe. And you can fool yourself into thinking that you can see what's going to be on the screen, but actually too many people intervene in the finished product, you're just a part of the process, so it's quite unlike a novel where you're in sole charge, as it were.
Interviewer:	Tom, there, unfortunately, we have to leave it. Thank you …

[pause]

tone

Now you'll hear the recording again.

[The recording is repeated.]

[pause]

That's the end of Part Three.
Now turn to Part Four.

[pause]

PART 4   *Part Four*

Part Four consists of two tasks. You'll hear five short extracts in which people are reading from their autobiographies. Look at Task One. For questions 21 to 25, choose from the list A to H what each speaker is saying. Now look at Task Two. For questions 26 to 30, choose from the list A to H the feeling each speaker expresses. While you listen you must complete both tasks. You now have 45 seconds to look at Part Four.

[pause]

tone

[pause]

Speaker One: So there I was, all of a sudden it had all happened for me. All those years of struggle, to become 'an overnight success'. 'Lucky you!' my friends said, but luck didn't come into it, just perseverance in the face of all the rejection. And did it all seem worth it now? Now that I'd finally made it? Well, I didn't have much time to get carried away with it all. The record company wanted the next record. How was I going to follow it? Had I used up all my inspiration? Was I just a 'one-hit wonder', destined to be instantly forgotten? These thoughts kept me awake at night.

[pause]

Speaker Two: That day the phone never stopped ringing. Everyone wanted to know, 'Have you seen the paper?' Well, imagine what it's like to have your photograph plastered all over the front page with a story like that. 'TV star in police enquiry' it said and the article was full of things they'd just made up, and plain lies. Well, it hadn't happened to me before and I wasn't really ready for it, but I thought, 'Well, that's the way it goes. It's the price of fame, as they say. I won't even bother denying such a load of rubbish.' So I didn't react and pretty soon the whole thing had blown over.

[pause]

Speaker Three: I suppose I first realised what had happened when I went to my regular restaurant and instead of showing me to 'my table', the head waiter asked me if I'd booked. I suppose most people would have got depressed but in a funny sort of way I was glad. I thought, 'I've made my money and now there's a new generation of comedians taking over and people don't find me funny any more.' But I'm not going to miss it, all those people coming up to you in shops and expecting you to be funny all the time, all those idiots telling you jokes in restaurants. Oh, it'll be bliss not to have to put up with that any more.

[pause]

Speaker Four: So then I had to tell the others. We'd known each other since we were kids, we'd formed the band in our teens and now I was going to tell them I was going solo. But I knew it was exactly the right thing for me to do at that time. We were right at the top and the only way was down. And anyway, I'd got the feeling they'd had about enough – all that touring, it was wearing us all out. So I figured they wouldn't take it badly – in a way they'd be glad I'd made the decision for them. And I was looking forward to taking up a new challenge.

[pause]

Speaker Five: The next day it began to sink in. My big break, my first major role in a major film and I'd let it go. It was a strange feeling. I mean, I should have been devastated but the more I thought about it, the more I realised they'd only been taking me for a ride. Just because I was a relative unknown, they'd thought they could get me on the cheap. Well, I thought, nobody treats me like that. I was right to tell them what they could do with their lousy offer. What a cheek! I almost rang them back to give them a piece of my mind but I thought better of it. Still, better parts'll come my way soon, I said to myself, and I was right.

[pause]

tone

Now you'll hear the recording again.

[The recording is repeated.]

[pause]

That's the end of Part Four.
*There'll now be a pause of **five minutes** for you to **copy your answers onto the separate answer sheet**. Be sure to follow the numbering of all the questions. I'll remind you when there's one minute left, so that you're sure to finish in time.*

[Teacher, pause the recording here for five minutes. Remind your students when they have one minute left.]

That's the end of the test. Please stop now. Your supervisor will now collect all the question papers and answer sheets.

Test 3 Key

Paper 1   Reading (1 hour 15 minutes)

Part 1

1 C   2 C   3 B   4 D   5 B   6 C

Part 2

7 C   8 F   9 A   10 G   11 D   12 E

Part 3

13 C   14 D   15 C   16 C   17 B   18 A   19 B

Part 4

20 B   21 C   22 D   23 A   24 A   25 B   26 C   27 B
28 A   29 B   30 C   31 A   32 B   33 D   34 C

Paper 2   Writing (1 hour 30 minutes)

Part 1

Question 1

Content (points covered)
For a Band 3 or above, the candidate's **report** must:
• explain what the writer thought about the holiday
• say whether the writer recommends the holiday to others
• give reasons.

Organisation and cohesion
Clearly organised into paragraphs with appropriate linking devices.
Headings may be an advantage.

Range
Language of description, explanation and recommendation.
Vocabulary related to leisure and learning.

Appropriacy of register and format
Formal to unmarked. Must be consistent.

Target reader
Would be informed.

Part 2

Question 2

Content (points covered)
For Band 3 or above, the candidate's **article** must:
• discuss problems relating to either work, education or the environment
• relate this to young people in candidate's country.

Organisation and cohesion
Clearly organised into paragraphs with appropriate linking devices.

Range
Language of description and discussion.

Appropriacy of register and format
May mix registers if appropriate to approach taken by candidate.

Target reader
Would be informed.

Question 3

Content (points covered)
For Band 3 or above, the candidate's **reference** must:
• indicate how long they have known the person
• describe the person's character in detail
• explain why the person would be suitable for the job.

Organisation and cohesion
Clearly organised into paragraphs with appropriate linking devices.

Range
Language of description, explanation and recommendation.
Vocabulary related to character and work.

Appropriacy of register and format
Unmarked to formal. Must be consistent.

Target reader
Would be informed and consider application.

Question 4

Content (points covered)
For Band 3 or above, the candidate's **competition entry** must:
• describe one leisure facility they would like
• explain why it is needed
• state what they would like the leisure facility to provide
• explain which groups in the community would benefit.

Organisation and cohesion
Clearly organised into paragraphs with appropriate linking devices.

Range
Language of description, opinion and explanation.

Appropriacy of register and format
May mix registers if appropriate to approach taken by candidate.

Target reader
Would be informed.

Question 5 (a)

Content (points covered)
For Band 3 or above, the candidate's **essay** must:
- describe the strengths and weaknesses of two parent-child relationships in *Big Stone Gap*
- explain how each of these relationships could have been improved.

Organisation and cohesion
Clearly organised into paragraphs with appropriate linking devices.

Range
Language of description, explanation and opinion.
Vocabulary related to relationships.

Appropriacy of register and format
May mix registers if appropriate to approach taken by candidate.

Target reader
Would be informed.

Question 5 (b)

Content (points covered)
For Band 3 or above, the candidate's **review** must:
- comment on whether the candidate feels the book deserves to be called a thriller
- explain which scene the candidate found most thrilling.

Organisation and cohesion
Clearly organised into paragraphs with appropriate linking devices.

Range
Language of description, opinion and explanation.
Vocabulary related to description of stories and comment on a book.

Appropriacy of register and format
May mix registers if appropriate to approach taken by candidate.

Target reader
Would be informed.

Paper 3   Use of English (1 hour)

Part 1

1 B	2 A	3 C	4 C	5 A	6 A	7 A
8 D	9 B	10 C	11 D	12 A		

Part 2

13 at   14 of   15 whose   16 them / others / these   17 has   18 their
19 it   20 too   21 on   22 is   23 how   24 any   25 have
26 when / if   27 same

Part 3

28 enthusiasm   29 extraordinary   30 significance   31 dramatic   32 undertaken
33 actively   34 outstanding   35 foundation(s)   36 footsteps   37 insight

Part 4

38 see   39 well   40 count   41 high   42 met

Part 5

43 every chance | of getting / winning   44 apart from her sister / her sister apart | nobody
/ no one (else) [reverse order also possible]   45 because / as / since he was | short of
46 is / to be capable | of winning   47 explain why | she (had) made   48 did not / didn't
make (any) | reference to OR made no | reference to   49 her delight | Lucy was OR Lucy's
delight | she was   50 never occurred to Sam | to ask

Paper 4 Listening (approximately 40 minutes)

Part 1

1 B   2 B   3 C   4 A   5 B   6 A

Part 2

7 seventeenth / 17th   8 nature / (the) countryside   9 status symbol / symbol of status
10 tree planting / to plant (a) tree(s) / (the) planting of trees   11 (fruit and vegetable)
gardens / gardening / fruit(s) and vegetables   12 grass (land) (fields) / grasslands
13 (the) breeding / keeping (of) (the) animals / animal breeding / animal keeping / animal
husbandry   14 (traditional / common / contemporary) romantic (traditional)

Part 3

15 D   16 A   17 A   18 C   19 B   20 B

Part 4

21 B   22 F   23 H   24 E   25 D   26 F   27 E   28 B   29 H   30 C

Transcript   *This is the Cambridge Certificate in Advanced English Listening Test. Test Three.
I'm going to give you the instructions for this test. I'll introduce each part of the test
and give you time to look at the questions.*

At the start of each piece you'll hear this sound:

tone

You'll hear each piece twice.

*Remember, while you're listening, write your answers on the **question paper**. You'll have **five minutes** at the end of the test to **copy your answers onto the separate answer sheet**.*

There'll now be a pause. Please ask any questions now, because you must not speak during the test.

[pause]

PART 1   *Now open your question paper and look at Part One.*

[pause]

You'll hear three different extracts. For questions one to six, choose the answer (A, B or C) which fits best according to what you hear. There are two questions for each extract.

Extract 1   *You overhear two friends discussing the work of a well-known sculptor. Now look at questions one and two.*

[pause]

tone

Man:	I've just been to see a sculpture by the artist John Maxine. Have you heard of him?
Woman:	Mmm, there's one of his pieces in a park near me – the last time I saw it, some children were climbing all over it. Quite a contrast between their happy faces and his sorrowful figures, but then there's always something very emotional going on in his work. It's hard to find other examples in popular galleries and exhibitions, though. The curators don't seem to value him very much.
Man:	Really?
Woman:	Mmm – a pity.
Man:	Yeah, interestingly, the one I got to see had been used by another artist in a work of her own. She'd wrapped the whole thing in plastic, for some reason – not at all what the artist had intended, I'm sure. I reckon a principle of conservation should be that nothing is done to alter original works of art in public collections.
Woman:	But if the sculptor were still alive, I'm sure he'd have considered it. Maybe he'd think there was value in taking something familiar and changing it, to trigger new layers of meaning.
Man:	Well, yes, I know that *is* valuable but if the artist can't be consulted ...
Woman:	Even so ...

[pause]

tone

Now you'll hear the recording again.

[The recording is repeated.]

[pause]

Extract 2   *You overhear two friends, Jamie and Miriam, discussing Miriam's future trip to the Gambia, in West Africa. Now look at questions three and four.*

[pause]

tone

159

Jamie:	So you're off to the Gambia, Miriam!
Miriam:	Yes, this time next week I'll be sunning myself on that wonderful Atlantic beach. I haven't had a holiday for a year, remember? I need some wall-to-wall sunshine.
Jamie:	I think you'll find there's a bit more to it than that. You ought to get yourself a local guide or take a boat yourself and explore the traditional villages up river.
Miriam:	That sounds great – I might just do that. Anyway, I always wait till I arrive in a place before arranging any excursions – that way my money goes directly to the local people.
Jamie:	You don't want to simply line the pockets of the travel companies.
Miriam:	And there's always things to watch for, not to offend people. I mean, their whole culture's different.
Jamie:	Well, tourists can't be expected to know everything about the local customs, can they? One thing I think is crucial is to leave the place just as you find it – no fires, no litter, no tyremarks –
Miriam:	You're saying you can't cycle anywhere then?
Jamie:	Well, let's not argue about it. You'll have a great time in the Gambia anyway.

[pause]

tone

Now you'll hear the recording again.

[The recording is repeated.]

[pause]

Extract 3   *You hear part of an interview with a successful financial manager, Frank Ewert, who has just resigned from his company. Now look at questions five and six.*

[pause]

tone

Interviewer:	Frank, you're universally acknowledged as one of the best fund managers ever – you handle multi-million pound investments on behalf of individuals. What is it that's got you personally to where you are today?
Frank:	There's a strong element of competition in financial institutions worldwide – we're looking over our shoulders all the time – and we all strive to meet higher revenue targets every year – but those are things we all have in common. What I think I did was dare to be different, in finding sectors that *weren't* tried and tested. My company, Harveys International, are still reaping the benefits.
Interviewer:	But now you've left Harveys. Will your clients be upset at your deserting them?
Frank:	They have no reason to be, because I'm leaving them in the capable hands of my successor, Gaynor Wong. I've always greatly appreciated their long-term loyalty to me and my team. In future they'll want to make their own decisions about where to put their money, and I'm no longer involved in that, but Gaynor will obviously do her best to persuade them to keep their investments with Harveys.
Interviewer:	And what direction do you think you . . . *(fade)*

[pause]

tone

Now you'll hear the recording again.

[The recording is repeated.]

[pause]

That's the end of Part One.
Now turn to Part Two.

[pause]

PART 2 *Part Two*

You'll hear a tour guide talking to a group of visitors outside an historic country house. For questions 7 to 14, complete the sentences. You now have 45 seconds to look at Part Two.

[pause]

tone

Tour guide So, here we are at Newton House, a typical eighteenth-century English country house, set in its own beautiful park. Before we go inside, let's look at the park which really is a classic example of its type, with rolling grassland and scattered trees.

'Park' is a word we use a lot nowadays. But if you trace back the history of the park as an idea, it is actually something which came into being as recently as the seventeenth century. People in the fifteenth and sixteenth centuries wouldn't really have understood what a park was, the idea simply didn't exist.

But *our* ideas about the countryside have changed a lot since then too. People in past centuries knew about agriculture because most of the population was involved in it. But nature, in the sense of wild places, was seen as something dangerous. People wanted civilised, man-made landscapes that showed how the wilderness of nature could be made safe and beautiful. This was how parks began.

Well, only rich people had parks, and socially, parkland quickly became significant as a status symbol, first appearing near large country houses like this because it was where the richest people, the big landowners, lived. Also very symbolic socially was tree-planting because trees involved long-term investment. They express a confidence in the future, and so they were carefully planted in prominent positions.

What happened during the eighteenth century is that the park became even more important as a setting for a large house, and the fruit and vegetable gardens, which had always been attached to houses, became less significant, often hidden away to one side. This was because if the park was to clearly distinguish its owner as a wealthy person, it needed to be beautiful but not very productive.

The immediate surroundings of the house were predominantly grassland, therefore, not fields of crops; they would look too much like work. But that doesn't mean that the land was completely useless. Rich people often involved themselves in breeding animals, for example, which was regarded as a kind of acceptable form of agriculture, something more like a sport.

Later, in the nineteenth century, urban parks appeared, taking up some of the ideas of rural park design, and those coming from Romantic traditions, common at the time, of what represented the picturesque. These pretty corners in cities gradually came to be used for the recreation of growing urban populations. This was quite a different purpose from that of the country park, which could be seen as representing a kind of barrier around the rich who were increasingly wanting to distance themselves from local farming communities, as well as from the growing urban areas.

[pause]

tone

Now you'll hear the recording again.

[The recording is repeated.]

[pause]

That's the end of Part Two.
Now turn to Part Three.

[pause]

PART 3   *Part Three*

You'll hear an interview with a woman called Carol Jones, who cycled around the world. For questions 15 to 20, choose the answer (A, B, C or D) which fits best according to what you hear. You now have one minute to look at Part Three.

[pause]

tone

Interviewer: Now, Carol, you've built up something of a reputation for yourself as, I hope you won't mind me saying, the grandmother of cycling. After all, you didn't actually take to two wheels until you took early retirement from a career as a head teacher. Was there an inspirational moment when you realised that travel on two wheels was what you'd been seeking?

Carol: Yes. I was on a package holiday, in the school holidays, and I was in a coach travelling across a desert in India and I looked out of the coach window and I saw this man. He was a solitary man and he was pedalling across the immensity of the desert. And I suddenly thought: 'I don't want to be looking at the world through a window'. And that reaction came as a complete surprise. I'd never been the least bit sporty and I didn't even have a bicycle. But at that moment I knew I was going to cycle across India. Later on I thought: 'Well, while I'm at it, I might as well cycle round the world.'

Interviewer: Surely you didn't just set off right away?

Carol: It took me five years to summon up the courage after that moment of enlightenment because it involved taking early retirement, and you know, it was such a major leap into the dark; there were times when I'd wake up in a cold sweat at night and I'd start having second thoughts about my chances of getting it off the ground. But once I began to think about the route, I decided to go London to London, west to east, it all began to fall into place. I had to have the bicycle custom built, and I went and told Condor cycles what I wanted to do and they saw to it for me. And it's still going strong. It's done about 70,000 kilometres.

Interviewer: Now there's not time to hear about all the places you visited, but tell us about people's reactions to you generally, you know as you cycled around?

Carol: Well, what struck me is that most countries have a strong tradition of hospitality and you're invited into people's homes. Of course in some places there was lots of bureaucracy, you know, at the borders. Officials couldn't understand what an old woman like me was doing on a bicycle. But in the main people were very intrigued by me, they said most women they knew of my age were at home looking after their grandchildren, so they didn't know what to make of me really.

Interviewer: So, what were some of the challenges you faced?

Carol:	Well, even though I had a smattering of some key languages, once I got out into country areas I found the local dialects impenetrable and I hadn't realized how much that would affect me psychologically. As far as the physical challenges are concerned, I actually got used to the mountains. I discovered that if I thought about doing it little by little, focusing on a tree not far off and then a particular rock, I could just about make it. What I never tired of was the variety of food – I never knew what to expect next.
Interviewer:	So Carol, all in all, why would you recommend a bicycle for travelling around the world?
Carol:	I think that because you look vulnerable, you're obviously no threat, so people take to you. You know, you go into a tea shop in the country in Asia, for example, and everybody else has come there on a bicycle too, so you're one of them. And some people say it's a great advantage that you don't have to share the experience with someone; that you just enjoy it under your own steam; that it's all a matter of determination and self-reliance. There's something in that too.
Interviewer:	Is there anything you'd do differently?
Carol:	Well, I realise that I missed a few golden opportunities en route, and got myself into needless difficulties at times, but you learn from those experiences, so there's no point crying over spilt milk. But I guess on a deeper level, I have been rather self-indulgent and there've been times since when I've wondered what was really behind it all – I ought to have known really, shouldn't I? People assume that I was raising money for good causes, and maybe I could've done, but sponsorship wasn't ever part of the plan, so I'm not going to start feeling guilty about it. But maybe if I was starting again, I'd consider that side of it more.
Interviewer:	And are more trips planned?
Carol:	Well yes. Actually, I'm just off to . . . [*fade*]

[pause]

tone

Now you'll hear the recording again.

[The recording is repeated.]

[pause]

That's the end of Part Three.
Now turn to Part Four.

[pause]

PART 4

Part Four

Part Four consists of two tasks. you'll hear five short extracts in which people are talking about the experience of winning a competition. Look at Task One. For questions 21 to 25, choose from the list A to H each speaker's present occupation. Now look at Task Two. For questions 26 to 30, choose from the list A to H the activity in which each speaker won a competition. While you listen you must complete both tasks. You now have 45 seconds to look at Part Four.

[pause]

tone

Speaker One:	I felt really proud when I won the competition. You expect it to be professional people with fancy qualifications who'd win, you know, solicitors or company executives, not someone like me who left school at sixteen and just does manual work. But that's it really. I need something to counteract the noise and tedium of the assembly line, where I don't have to think at all. After I've cooked for the family, I practise alone or with a friend. It's very quiet and you have to use your brain to plan your own moves and anticipate what your opponent will do. Now I've won, I'm thinking about writing a book to help beginners.

[pause]

Speaker Two:	I've never entered this before so I was really surprised to win a prize. I felt sure my friend Bob would win. His beans were much bigger and longer than mine. However, the judge said mine were straighter and more uniform. I love being outside after spending all day running a busy sales office. I used to play golf but it's time-consuming because I have to drive to the course first. While with this, I can just pop out the back door for ten minutes or so. It's good exercise and it relieves my stress after dealing with awkward customers on the phone. You need the skills of a politician now to keep everyone happy.

[pause]

Speaker Three:	I got a letter today, telling me I'd won second prize, which was a great thrill. My job got me started on all this. You see, I fly all over the world, to rather inhospitable regions sometimes, where the various construction sites are. So when I'm not needed to check that a design has been followed accurately or to redraft something, I can wander around. My knowledge of different countries and their history and geography has increased considerably. I wish I had some talent as a painter as some of the scenery and wildlife I've seen are breathtaking. Still, the next best thing is to capture it digitally. So that's what I do.

[pause]

Speaker Four:	My colleagues have no idea that I do this in my spare time. When I told them I'd won a competition, they assumed it was for cabbages or possibly a cake since I love being in the kitchen, especially in winter when my job quietens down. Actually, it's my job that started me off. When I'm outside, surrounded by flowers with wonderfully bright contrasting colours, I often think of precious stones – rubies, emeralds and so on. I was interested to see if I could use those to reflect the beauty of the natural world. Having worked in an engineering factory originally, I knew some of the basic techniques for metalwork, which helped.

[pause]

Speaker Five:	My job involves a lot of travelling, both around the country for meetings or to visit factories and businesses, particularly at election time. I also fly to other countries to improve my knowledge of their systems so we could try to introduce similar laws here. When I'm travelling, I do some sport to keep fit and relax by doing something creative. I'd love to do something artistic because I'm really into modern jewellery. I'd need a studio for that though, which isn't portable. But I have my laptop so, when I'm not drafting speeches, I have fun creating fiction, especially when there's a word-limit, based on unusual things that have happened in my career.

[pause]

tone

Now you'll hear the recording again.

[The recording is repeated.]

[pause]

That's the end of Part Four.
*There'll now be a pause of **five minutes** for you to **copy your answers onto the separate answer sheet.** Be sure to follow the numbering of all the questions. I'll remind you when there's one minute left, so that you're sure to finish in time.*

[Teacher, pause the recording here for five minutes. Remind your students when they have one minute left.]

That's the end of the test. Please stop now. Your supervisor will now collect all the question papers and answer sheets.

Test 4 Key

Paper 1   Reading (1 hour 15 minutes)

Part 1

1 B   2 A   3 D   4 A   5 D   6 C

Part 2

7 F   8 D   9 G   10 E   11 A   12 C

Part 3

13 C   14 C   15 A   16 A   17 D   18 D   19 B

Part 4

20 E   21 C   22 B   23 A / E   24 E / A   25 A   26 B   27 D
28 B   29 D   30 B   31 A   32 C   33 A   34 A

Paper 2   Writing (1 hour 30 minutes)

Part 1

Question 1

Content (points covered)
For a Band 3 or above, the candidate's **letter** must:
• say what was enjoyable about visit
• explain what was disappointing
• suggest ways to attract more visitors.

Organisation and cohesion
Clearly organised into paragraphs with appropriate linking devices.
Letter format with suitable opening and closing formulae.
Early reference to reason for writing.

Range
Language of description, explanation and suggestion.
Vocabulary related to tourism and museums.

Appropriacy of register and format
Formal to unmarked. Must be consistent.

Target reader
Would be informed.

Part 2

Question 2

Content (points covered)
For Band 3 or above, the candidate's **article** must:
• mention the impact of mobile phones
• discuss at least one type/example of **both** personal **and** business use
• refer to advantages **and** disadvantages of mobile phones.

Organisation and cohesion
Clearly organised into paragraphs with appropriate linking devices.
N.B. Letter format acceptable.

Range
Language of description and evaluation.
Vocabulary related to mobile phone use.

Appropriacy of register and format
Any, as long as consistent.

Target reader
Would be informed.

Question 3

Content (points covered)
For Band 3 or above, the candidate's **proposal** must:
• persuade reader that town is suitable for event
• comment on accommodation, transport and entertainment.

Organisation and cohesion
Clearly organised into paragraphs with appropriate linking devices.
Headings may be an advantage.

Range
Language of description, evaluation and persuasion.
Vocabulary related to leisure facilities.

Appropriacy of register and format
Any, as long as consistent.

Target reader
Would be informed.

Question 4

Content (points covered)
For Band 3 or above, the candidate's **information sheet** must give advice on:
• methods of study
• accommodation
• social life.

Organisation and cohesion
Clearly organised into paragraphs with appropriate linking devices.
Headings may be an advantage.

Range
Language of description and advice.
Vocabulary related to school and study.

Appropriacy of register and format
Any, as long as consistent.

Target reader
Would be informed.

Question 5 (a)

Content (points covered)
For Band 3 or above, the candidate's **article** must:
- comment on two of the scenes and how the participants in them would have been feeling
- explain why the scenes made a particularly strong impression on the candidate.

Organisation and cohesion
Clearly organised into paragraphs with appropriate linking devices.

Range
Language of description, opinion and explanation.
Vocabulary related to description of stories and comment on a book.

Appropriacy of register and format
May mix registers if appropriate to approach taken by candidate.

Target reader
Would be informed.

Question 5 (b)

Content (points covered)
For Band 3 or above, the candidate's **report** must:
- briefly describe *In the Frame*
- explain whether it would be (a) useful and (b) enjoyable as a book/film to study in class.

Organisation and cohesion
Clearly organised into paragraphs with appropriate linking devices.

Range
Language of description, opinion and explanation.
Vocabulary related to description of stories and comment on a book/film.

Appropriacy of register and format
May mix registers if appropriate to approach taken by candidate.

Target reader
Would be informed.

Paper 3　Use of English (1 hour)

Part 1

1 A　　2 A　　3 C　　4 D　　5 A　　6 B　　7 A　　8 C　　9 A　　10 C
11 B　　12 D

Part 2

13 all　　14 in　　15 but / only / yet　　16 them　　17 or / nor　　18 his
19 where / when　　20 and　　21 with / for　　22 to　　23 it　　24 on
25 Had / Has　　26 too　　27 (al)though

Part 3

28 musicians 29 residents 30 belongings 31 undiscovered 32 geographical
33 connections 34 considerably 35 picturesque 36 evidence 37 handful

Part 4

38 order 39 strong 40 passed 41 keep 42 land

Part 5

43 no intention | of going 44 Fred's failure | to answer 45 you should have / 've | lent
46 will have been | in England for 47 how hard | they tried / struggled OR how much hard
work | they did 48 it clear (that) | she was not / wasn't 49 you will / 'll find it | (very / too /
particularly) difficult 50 he would ring | the moment (that)

Paper 4 Listening (approximately 40 minutes)

Part 1

1 C 2 B 3 B 4 C 5 C 6 B

Part 2

7 Far Horizons / far horizons 8 alone / on your own 9 tools / equipment / (you need)
10 above freezing / above 0°C (centigrade) / above zero 11 (effective)(some) heating / heat
12 (enormous) tree trunks 13 polar bear(s) 14 (a) package tour(s) / (a) package
holiday(s) / (tourist) packages / a package

Part 3

15 A 16 B 17 D 18 D 19 C 20 B

Part 4

21 G 22 A 23 D 24 F 25 B 26 D 27 C 28 H 29 B 30 F

Transcript *This is the Cambridge Certificate in Advanced English, Listening Test. Test Four.*
I'm going to give you the instructions for this test.
I'll introduce each part of the test and give you time to look at the questions.

At the start of each piece you'll hear this sound:

tone

You'll hear each piece twice.

*Remember, while you're listening, write your answers on the **question paper**. You'll*
*have five minutes at the end of the test to **copy your answers onto the separate***
***answer sheet**.*

There'll now be a pause. Please ask any questions now, because you must not speak during the test.

[pause]

PART 1

Now open your question paper and look at Part One.

[pause]

You'll hear three different extracts. For questions one to six, choose the answer (A, B or C) which fits best according to what you hear. There are two questions for each extract.

Extract 1

You hear part of a radio programme about making a cake called a Swiss Roll. Now look at questions one and two.

[pause]

tone

Woman: Ed, I hear you made a brilliant Swiss Roll the other day.
Man: I know, it was really good!
Woman: How did that happen?
Man: Well, I'd had the recipe for ages in a folder where I keep all the foodie articles from magazines and so on. And I don't know why but I suddenly had an urge to make a Swiss Roll, so I rushed out and got myself the right sort of thing to cook it in. Then I dashed back to the kitchen, which fortunately happened to be in an unusually tidy state from a previous clean-up. And I made the Swiss Roll.
Woman: Wow!
Man: Yep. And you know, it was a good feeling – beating the eggs and smoothing the mixture and all that – and thinking, I've never done this before. I did wonder at the time, I mean how do you *know* it's going to rise and look gorgeous? And it wasn't all plain sailing. The trickiest bit is rolling it up with its filling inside.
Woman: But hey! It worked.
Man: And I have to tell you it was delicious.

[pause]

tone

Now you'll hear the recording again.

[The recording is repeated.]

[pause]

Extract 2

You hear part of an interview with the novelist Joanna Marley, who is talking about the notebooks she uses. Now look at questions three and four.

[pause]

tone

Interviewer: So how important is your notebook in the writing process?
Joanna: Oh, I'm the queen of notebooks! I've just bought a new one. They're always essential in the research process and it's harder to start without one. Although this time I've already begun making research notes on my laptop. But I tend to go for notebooks with covers that are connected in some way to what I'm writing and I've found them hard to find. This time I struck lucky, though – my new novel's about a shell collector, and I soon found a notebook that evokes the seaside, so that's really made me want to research the topic further.

Interviewer:	And do notebooks remain important once you've started writing?
Joanna:	Well, some writers regard them as reassuring, so there might be some anxiety if one went missing. But *I* was actually advised once by a writing tutor to leave my notebook aside once the research was finished. That's turned out to be very good advice because although I love writing notes and doing the research, I find that consulting one after I've started inhibits my creativity . . .
Interviewer:	Mmm, I can understand that . . . (*fade*)

[pause]

tone

Now you'll hear the recording again.

[The recording is repeated.]

[pause]

Extract 3   *You hear a man and a woman discussing professional tennis players. Now look at questions five and six.*

[pause]

tone

Man:	You been following the tennis on TV?
Woman:	Yeah! I really don't know how they play so well under such stressful conditions. The crowds must be pretty distracting – especially if they're cheering for your opponent!
Man:	Mmm, but you get that in basketball matches too, don't you?
Woman:	Well, yes – it's just a bit annoying, really. But at least you're in a team. These players are alone on court – alone for hours; must be awful – I'd need reassurance from *someone* during a match.
Man:	Mmm, me too.
Woman:	Then there's the weather that can cause a match to be delayed or called off – though I'm used to that where I come from!
Man:	I guess so! But remember, they *are* professionals, so they're good at preparing mentally beforehand – that's needed in any profession, after all. I've read, though, that they're taught to visualise difficult situations and then imagine how to deal with them – must be hard to apply that just when you need it. And ideally they should keep their heads, too, though I've often seen players lose control just within sight of winning.
Woman:	I suppose they *are* only human.

[pause]

tone

Now you'll hear the recording again.

[The recording is repeated.]

[pause]

That's the end of Part One.
Now turn to Part Two.

[pause]

PART 2

Part Two

You'll hear a journalist called Peter Smith talking about a trip he made to the Arctic seas around the North Pole. For questions 7 to 14, complete the sentences. You now have 45 seconds to look at Part Two.

[pause]

tone

Peter Smith: I can't pinpoint the exact moment when I made the decision to embark on my sailing expedition to the North Pole. The previous summer I'd come across a book entitled *Far Horizons* which suggested that a voyage of this kind was a unique experience – and everyone should try it once! So, I put on three layers of clothing and set off in my boat in July with a small crew to sail to the Arctic seas near the North Pole. I felt it was time I went in search of adventure!

I'd been told that sailing there shouldn't present any more problems than you'd expect sailing round the seas in the north of Britain. Well, initially that was true. But there were differences. The most noticeable is that, up there in the Arctic seas, you have the impression of being alone. So, if anything breaks down or goes wrong – for example, one of our large front cabin windows shattered in the gale we encountered on our first night – you have to have all the tools you need. We would have been very cold and wet if we hadn't had the means to make a solid repair. The second big difference is the temperature. In the winter in those seas, things can get down to minus fifty degrees. In the summer, it's much warmer and the surface sea water is always above freezing but the air temperature never rises much above ten degrees. This all means two things. The first is that the cabin of your boat must have effective heating. The second is that you must have proper outdoor clothing. Another difference is that you meet some things that aren't found on a normal sailing trip. Not surprisingly, we met gigantic lumps of ice which had broken off icebergs, and occasionally we saw enormous tree trunks on the sea. We really weren't sure what they were doing there!

They do say that in those seas you can even spot polar bears, which are reported to be very dangerous if disturbed. Unfortunately, we weren't able to catch sight of one, although we did see whales.

For all this effort, though, you're rewarded with a trip to a true wilderness, which can be reached in your very own boat. More than 250,000 tourists visit this area each year, but in order to protect the environment, and because of the difficulty in getting there, most of the tourism takes the form of package tours. These have only limited access to certain unrestricted areas. But, in your own boat, you can have the whole area to yourself!

[pause]

tone

Now you'll hear the recording again.

[The recording is repeated.]

[pause]

That's the end of Part Two.
Now turn to Part Three.

[pause]

PART 3   *Part Three*

You'll hear part of an interview with Norman Cowley, a well-known novelist and biographer. For questions 15 to 20, choose the answer (A, B, C or D) which fits best according to what you hear. You now have one minute to look at Part Three.

[pause]

tone

Interviewer:	With us today to discuss his career we have Norman Cowley, renowned novelist and biographer. So let's start at the beginning, Norman. You did say, some years ago, that you began high on the mountain, only to go down sharply while others were passing you on the way up. Do you think now, when you look back at your first novel, that it had anything that you were not able to recapture later?
Norman Cowley:	You can't write a worthwhile book, or you can't continue to be a reasonable writer if you start recapturing what you've done earlier. So there are all sorts of positive things in my first book that I'll never achieve again – the immediacy of it, the easiness of the dialogue, the kind of stylistic elegance that comes from not trying to be too sophisticated. But, on the other hand, I wouldn't want to repeat it.
Interviewer:	Now, after the tremendous success of that first novel, your second one was pretty much damned by the critics.
Norman Cowley:	Oh, more than damned. It was torn apart!
Interviewer:	Well, now, that must have hurt, probably more than anything subsequently.
Norman Cowley:	It was shocking, because, and you know this is going to sound silly, but I couldn't believe the intensity of the attack on it. I remember one awful review by a longstanding, distinguished critic, who was uncharacteristically attempting to be witty, I suspect. He wrote that the book was 'paceless, tasteless, graceless.' Now it certainly had its faults but er . . . it had pace, it had its own kind of taste in tune with the youth culture of the time, and I like to think it had some grace. It was almost as if the reviewer had deliberately set out to pick the few good things he could find in the book and wreck them too. It was a demolition job.
Interviewer:	But did this rejection push you in a different direction?
Norman Cowley:	It left me very confused. I thought maybe I should give up and become something else, but I didn't know what. So I wandered around and finally started thinking about the next book, *The Green Wood*. Of course you get good reviews too, which give you hope, and the bad ones toughen you. Finally after many, many years, you realise that it's part of it. In a way, it's a pruning process. It cuts down all but the people who are really driven to be writers. So there are far more people who write two novels than six or seven.
Interviewer:	After a while, people began to see some autobiographical content in your fiction. Was that fair?
Norman Cowley:	It was half fair. You don't ever put someone into a book completely. You don't dare because if you do, you've got a dull character. The point is that if you put people that you know very well, like your wife or children, into a book, they're real for you already, so you don't have to create them. So they say a few things that they say every day and they're real for you, but not for anyone else. It's better if you change them. I love taking people and transforming them to a degree by, say, putting them in an occupation they don't have and so on.
Interviewer:	And what do you think about some of the novels written today with their extremely violent plots?

Norman Cowley:	I don't care what characters do in a novel. I'm willing to read about the worst human monster, provided the novelist can make that person come alive. A novel should enable you to learn more about the depths of human nature. Some of today's violent novels don't do that. There's no inner voyage. The writing's descriptive but not revealing. Probably there's such a thing as 'going too far', but only if you don't fulfil the prescription. You can go as far as you want but your imagination has to be equal to it.
Interviewer:	So the novel is still mainly a kind of psychological journey?
Norman Cowley:	Well, it can be many things: a riddle, a game or a wonderful revolution of language. I would hate to say novels have to be *one* thing, but the key is that they should illuminate human experience in a dramatic way. Otherwise why read them? You're going to get a better, swiftly-paced, modern narrative on the average TV show.
Interviewer:	Now, in your selection of subjects for biographical treatment, is there one aspect of all these people which attracted you? (*fade*) . . .

[pause]

tone

Now you'll hear the recording again.

[The recording is repeated.]

[pause]

That's the end of Part Three.
Now turn to Part Four.

PART 4	*Part Four*
	Part Four consists of two tasks. You'll hear five short extracts in which people are talking about the means of escape they use to cope with the demands of their working lives. Look at Task One. For questions 21 to 25, choose from the list A to H what each speaker finds demanding about their work. Now look at Task Two. For questions 26 to 30, choose from the list A to H what attracts the speakers to their different means of escape. While you listen you must complete both tasks. You now have 45 seconds to look at Part Four.

[pause]

tone

Speaker One:	I enjoy speed in every walk of life. Perhaps it's my weakness but I feel that time's so precious you mustn't waste it. That's why my car's my means of escape. I've always loved the sense of danger when driving fast cars and, if I didn't own the transport company I work in, I'd probably be a racing driver! The trouble is that because of the company's high profile, I'm often recognised. Now that's where the car comes in. I rarely take passengers or use it for any practical purpose. I just get in it and drive for hours. When I'm old and grey, I don't want to have any regrets. I don't want to think I didn't take advantage of the opportunities life offered me!

[pause]

Speaker Two: The garden was a wilderness when we moved into our present house. As a youngster, I'd always wanted a tree house in the garden and now it seems that I've built the deluxe version. It stands on stilts in the corner of the garden where nothing would grow. It even has a balcony and a light inside it! I don't know what I'd do if I didn't have it to escape to. You see, being an opera singer is an athletic pursuit and you have to train like an athlete for it. Once I get on stage, I'm swept along by the sheer feeling of commitment I have to what I do. You have to have access to grand passions to be able to live the part . . . which is great, but the need to switch off is even greater.

[pause]

Speaker Three: I've been going to watch Rugby football for over 25 years now. The club is totally amateur. There are no spectator stands and it's absolutely freezing in winter. The crowds vary between two and three hundred, though, depending on the fixture. But as soon as I walk into the ground, I completely switch off from the day-to-day pressure of the bank where I work as managing director – even if the game gets a bit lively sometimes! You see, I believe team games give you a better insight into what life is all about: that you have to take the knocks as well as give them, and that you can achieve more by working together than you can as an individual.

[pause]

Speaker Four: My means of escape isn't a solitary place. It's the study area part of our first floor living room and, with five-year-old twins and four older children, it's what you might call a place with quite a lot of hubbub. I sit here at the end of a long day and drink tea. Everyone near and dear to me comes in and out and talks about what they've been doing. My days are always busy because I work as a consultant in a hospital and every Tuesday I have a special clinic in the evenings, so I'm absolutely worn out most of the time. It's being at home that enables me to recharge my batteries.

[pause]

Speaker Five: There's a ranch in the US which I love going to. You ride in the morning in groups according to your ability and in the afternoons there are lawn games or whatever. You live in small cabins, which are comfortable rather than luxurious, and you eat good, plain food. It's so different from being a chief executive of an oil company, and I find it really relaxing. You see, when the company was originally founded in 1886, it took four months to get a message from the Far East. Now people are checking the stock market every two seconds and asking what you're going to do about so-and-so. Soon everything will be screened directly into your brain. You'll close your eyes and see the price of shares!

[pause]

Now you'll hear the recording again.

tone

[The recording is repeated.]

[pause]

That's the end of Part Four.

*There'll now be a pause of **five minutes** for you to **copy your answers onto the separate answer sheet.** Be sure to follow the numbering of all the questions. I'll remind you when there's one minute left, so that you're sure to finish in time.*

[Teacher, pause the recording here for five minutes. Remind your students when they have one minute left.]

That's the end of the test. Please stop now. Your supervisor will now collect all the question papers and answer sheets.

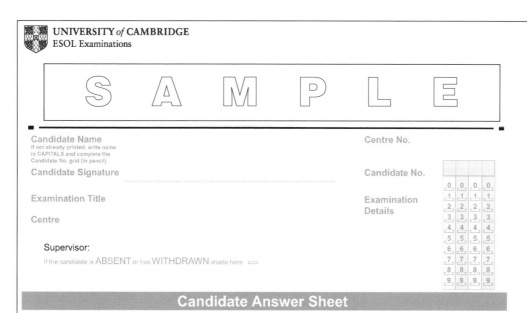

UNIVERSITY *of* **CAMBRIDGE**
ESOL Examinations

S A M P L E

Candidate Name
If not already printed, write name
in CAPITALS and complete the
Candidate No. grid (in pencil).

Candidate Signature

Examination Title

Centre

Supervisor:
If the candidate is ABSENT or has WITHDRAWN shade here ▭

Centre No.

Candidate No.

Examination Details

0 0 0 0
1 1 1 1
2 2 2 2
3 3 3 3
4 4 4 4
5 5 5 5
6 6 6 6
7 7 7 7
8 8 8 8
9 9 9 9

Candidate Answer Sheet

Instructions

Use a PENCIL (B or HB).

Mark ONE letter for each question.

For example, if you think B is the right answer to the question, mark your answer sheet like this:

0 A [B] C D E F G H

Rub out any answer you wish to change using an eraser.

1	A B C D E F G H	21 A B C D E F G H
2	A B C D E F G H	22 A B C D E F G H
3	A B C D E F G H	23 A B C D E F G H
4	A B C D E F G H	24 A B C D E F G H
5	A B C D E F G H	25 A B C D E F G H
6	A B C D E F G H	26 A B C D E F G H
7	A B C D E F G H	27 A B C D E F G H
8	A B C D E F G H	28 A B C D E F G H
9	A B C D E F G H	29 A B C D E F G H
10	A B C D E F G H	30 A B C D E F G H
11	A B C D E F G H	31 A B C D E F G H
12	A B C D E F G H	32 A B C D E F G H
13	A B C D E F G H	33 A B C D E F G H
14	A B C D E F G H	34 A B C D E F G H
15	A B C D E F G H	35 A B C D E F G H
16	A B C D E F G H	36 A B C D E F G H
17	A B C D E F G H	37 A B C D E F G H
18	A B C D E F G H	38 A B C D E F G H
19	A B C D E F G H	39 A B C D E F G H
20	A B C D E F G H	40 A B C D E F G H

© UCLES 2009 Photocopiable

177

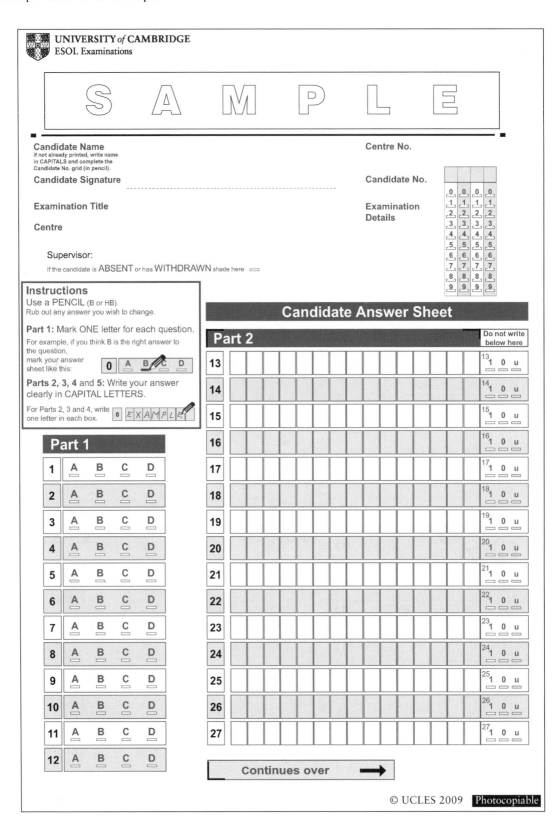

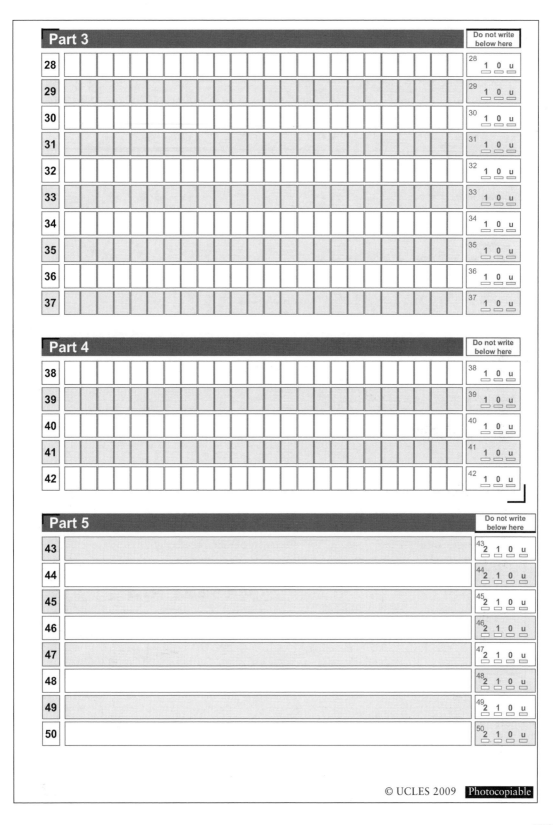

Part 3

Do not write below here

28		28 1 0 u
29		29 1 0 u
30		30 1 0 u
31		31 1 0 u
32		32 1 0 u
33		33 1 0 u
34		34 1 0 u
35		35 1 0 u
36		36 1 0 u
37		37 1 0 u

Part 4

Do not write below here

38		38 1 0 u
39		39 1 0 u
40		40 1 0 u
41		41 1 0 u
42		42 1 0 u

Part 5

Do not write below here

43		43 2 1 0 u
44		44 2 1 0 u
45		45 2 1 0 u
46		46 2 1 0 u
47		47 2 1 0 u
48		48 2 1 0 u
49		49 2 1 0 u
50		50 2 1 0 u

Sample answer sheet: Paper 4

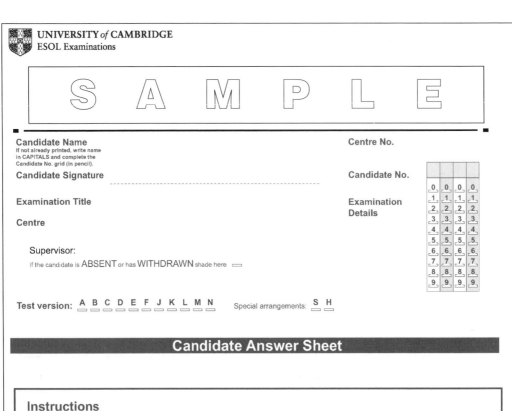

UNIVERSITY *of* **CAMBRIDGE**
ESOL Examinations

S A M P L E

Candidate Name
If not already printed, write name
in CAPITALS and complete the
Candidate No. grid (in pencil).

Candidate Signature

Examination Title

Centre

Supervisor:
If the candidate is ABSENT or has WITHDRAWN shade here

Test version: A B C D E F J K L M N   Special arrangements: S H

Centre No.

Candidate No.

Examination
Details

0	0	0	0
1	1	1	1
2	2	2	2
3	3	3	3
4	4	4	4
5	5	5	5
6	6	6	6
7	7	7	7
8	8	8	8
9	9	9	9

Candidate Answer Sheet

Instructions

Use a PENCIL (B or HB).
Rub out any answer you wish to change using an eraser.

Parts 1, 3 and **4:**
Mark ONE letter for each question.

For example, if you think **B** is the
right answer to the question, mark
your answer sheet like this:

Part 2:
Write your answer clearly in CAPITAL LETTERS.

Write one letter or number in each box.
If the answer has more than one word, leave one
box empty between words.

For example:

Turn this sheet over to start.

© UCLES 2009 · Photocopiable

180

Part 1

1	A	B	C
2	A	B	C
3	A	B	C
4	A	B	C
5	A	B	C
6	A	B	C

Part 2 (Remember to write in CAPITAL LETTERS or numbers)

Do not write below here

7		7 1 0 u
8		8 1 0 u
9		9 1 0 u
10		10 1 0 u
11		11 1 0 u
12		12 1 0 u
13		13 1 0 u
14		14 1 0 u

Part 3

15	A	B	C	D
16	A	B	C	D
17	A	B	C	D
18	A	B	C	D
19	A	B	C	D
20	A	B	C	D

Part 4

21	A	B	C	D	E	F	G	H
22	A	B	C	D	E	F	G	H
23	A	B	C	D	E	F	G	H
24	A	B	C	D	E	F	G	H
25	A	B	C	D	E	F	G	H
26	A	B	C	D	E	F	G	H
27	A	B	C	D	E	F	G	H
28	A	B	C	D	E	F	G	H
29	A	B	C	D	E	F	G	H
30	A	B	C	D	E	F	G	H